Vincent van Gogh and the Birth of Cloisonism

AN OVERVIEW

Paul Gauguin

Louis Anquetin

Emile Bernard

Henri de Toulouse-Lautrec

Jakob Meyer de Haan

Charles Laval

Maurice Denis

Paul Sérusier

BOGOMILA WELSH-OVCHAROV

Art Gallery of Ontario

Musée des beaux-arts de l'Ontario

Toronto / Canada

January 24 – March 22, 1981

ALL RIGHTS RESERVED

ISBN 0-919876-71-4

GRAPHIC DESIGN: FRANK NEWFELD

Photography, unless otherwise credited, by Photographic Services, Art Gallery of Ontario

Typeset in Bauer Bodoni by Trigraph, Toronto

Printed and bound by Ashton Potter Ltd., Toronto

Vincent van Gogh
and the Birth of Cloisonism

has received
the generous support of

Ontario Ministry of
Culture and Recreation

The Weston Group

Several Members of
the Art Gallery of Ontario

FRONTISPIECE:

Vincent van Gogh (Dutch, 1853-1890)
Self Portrait with Straw Hat, 1887
oil on pasteboard: 41 × 33 cm
Rijksmuseum Vincent van Gogh, Amsterdam

THE COVER:

Vincent van Gogh (Dutch, 1853-1890)
*Still Life: Vase with Iris Against a
Yellow Background*, St. Rémy, May 1890
oil on canvas, 92 × 73.5 cm
Rijksmuseum Vincent van Gogh, Amsterdam

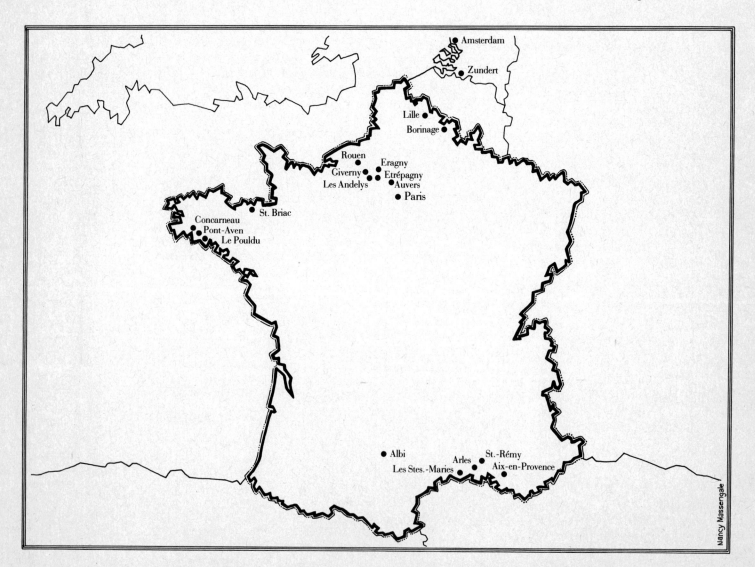

1.
Vincent van Gogh (1853-1890)
Agostina Segatori: In the Café Le Tambourin
c. February-March 1888
oil on canvas: 55.5 × 46.5 cm
Lent by the Rijksmuseum Vincent van Gogh,
Amsterdam

The sitter is Agostina Segatori, a one-time model
for various well-known artists of the period,
including Camille Corot. Van Gogh, who during
the first half of 1887 had formed a liaison with
Agostina, depicted her seated in her famous
bohemian café *Le Tambourin* on the Boulevard
de Clichy in Montmartre. The artist forcefully
captures her animal sensuality and melancholy
modernity as she leans on a tambourin-shaped
table, smoking a cigarette and wearing her
characteristic Neapolitan costume. Beside her to
the left, van Gogh has placed a folded parasol, as
often found in prints of Japanese actresses. This
painting can be considered a tribute to Degas'
Absinthe Drinker, in terms of style and also for
the Japanist raking-angle backdrop which Degas
above all others had introduced into modern
French painting. Behind this worldly Italian,
Vincent significantly commemorates not his own
art but that of Japan, making reference to the
now famous exhibition of Japanese prints which
he had organized early in spring 1887 for display
at the café and which he later credited with
having influenced Bernard and Anquetin toward
simplification of their respective art.

Preface

Vincent van Gogh and the Birth of Cloisonism is the most art-historically significant international exhibition to be shown in a Canadian gallery in at least the last decade. There are two fundamental reasons for its importance:

First through the generosity of a number of lenders, and especially that of the Rijksmuseum Vincent van Gogh, Amsterdam, the Art Gallery of Ontario has been able to assemble over 100 Post-Impressionist masterworks.

Secondly, these works will be seen together for the first, and probably last, time in a new historical perspective provided by the original research and thesis of a Canadian scholar, Dr. Bogomila Welsh.

The thesis, and the exhibition which illustrates it, explores the relationship of a great Dutch artist, Vincent van Gogh, to a particular tendency within French painting during the late 1880s. This emphasized, at the expense of traditional perspective and modelling in the round, a structure of strong contour lines filled in by flattened areas of bright colour. The term "cloisonism," derived from a popular form of medieval enamel work, was first applied to the art of Louis Anquetin, who had developed his personal style in close association with such colleagues as Henri de Toulouse-Lautrec, Vincent van Gogh and especially Emile Bernard, who inspired the adoption of Cloisonism by Paul Gauguin. The exhibition also investigates the importance of Neo-Impressionism to the development of Cloisonism and its repercussions within the Nabi and Art Nouveau movements.

The exhibition includes approximately forty-five works by van Gogh, half that number by each of Bernard and Gauguin and proportionately lesser representations of Anquetin and Toulouse-Lautrec. Due to their status on the periphery of the Cloisonist development, such artists as Charles Laval, Paul Sérusier, Meyer de Haan and Maurice Denis are represented by only a few examples each. The majority of items in the show are paintings. An accompanying body of watercolours, drawings and graphics has been included to amplify the thesis.

Of course, the organization of such an exhibition is complex, requiring long-term planning. Indeed, this exhibition was proposed early in 1976 by Dr. Richard Wattenmaker, at that time Chief Curator of the Art Gallery of Ontario, as a result of his interest in the research being undertaken by Dr. Welsh – research that was to demand her commitment for a full ten years. Dr. Welsh, as Guest Curator, went far beyond the usual responsibilities of such an appointment which include the selection of the works to be shown and the writing of the catalogue. Dr. Welsh orchestrated the negotiations for many of the loans, many of which involved face-to-face meetings with the lenders in various parts of the world.

Nor could the exhibition be realized without full co-operation between the Rijksmuseum Vincent van Gogh and the Art Gallery of Ontario. The collaboration of these two institutions demonstrates once again the close ties that exist between Canada and the Netherlands and the twinned cities, Toronto and Amsterdam. The Rijksmuseum Vincent van Gogh, under the General Directorship of Dr. Simon H. Levie and the Directorship of Dr. Johannes van der Wolk, has made an extraordinary and essential loan of major van Gogh paintings and drawings and works by other artists which form the core of the show.

We must also express our thanks to the 40 lenders, both private and institutional, from 8 countries, who have graciously entrusted their treasures to us. It is the good faith and generosity of these lenders that has made the success of the exhibition possible.

It should I think be recorded that almost exactly at the mid-point of 1980 we were beset with such financial difficulties as almost forced cancellation of the show. While planning for the exhibition began some four years ago, it was only during the six or seven months prior to the Toronto opening that the impact of extraordinary prices for major works on the world art market was felt. Costs that could not have been foreseen presented exceptional financial problems. We are therefore most grateful for the timely, special support of the Government of Ontario through the Ministry of Culture and Recreation. In addition we are deeply indebted to The Weston Group and to several Members of the Gallery, who wish to remain anonymous, for their generous sponsorship.

Finally, I should like to make a comment about this particular publication because it is somewhat different to the sort normally published by this Gallery for an exhibition.

An exhibition of the academic order of *Vincent van Gogh and the Birth of Cloisonism* demands a major scholarly catalogue. Such a catalogue is close to publication, delayed only by the late agreement on some of the loans. It was also recognized that this exhibition would have very broad public appeal and consequently very high attendance. It is for that large interested audience that this book has been prepared. Our aim has been to enhance the value of the exhibition by introducing the visitor to the thesis and to do so in a book that will find a place in the visitor's library.

WILLIAM J. WITHROW
Director, Art Gallery of Ontario

2.
Vincent van Gogh
Japonaiserie: The Courtesan (after Kesai Eisen)
late 1887
oil on canvas: 105 × 61 cm
Lent by the Rijksmuseum Vincent van Gogh,
Amsterdam

Van Gogh's deep admiration for Japanese art is documented within the artist's *oeuvre* by his *Portrait of Père Tanguy* (pl. 11) and by three copies after Japanese prints. By the summer of 1887 his rich personal collection of Japanese prints constantly presented him with new ideas in the simplification of colour and line. Of the three copies after Japanese prints, the *Japonaiserie: The Courtesan* remains his most monumental work. The figure was inspired by a reproduction of a print of the Oiran (Courtesan) by Kesai Eisen which appeared in reproduction on the cover of a special issue of *Paris Illustré* (May 1886) dedicated to Japan. Van Gogh transferred an enlarged version of the *Oiran* figure onto this canvas. However accurately he preserved the linear details of the kimono and facial features, Vincent departs radically from the original colour scheme by inventing a chromatically brilliant range of colour complementaries. Several back-ground motifs of frogs and cranes in their aquarian surroundings have been synthesized from various other Japanese sources. Van Gogh derives great stimulus for the cloisonist style from such researches into the highly coloured flat-surfaced decorative art of Japanese prints. He consciously strove to capture the essence of oriental art within his own personal view of Western society.

Acknowledgments

When in 1976 Dr. Richard Wattenmaker suggested that I undertake an exhibition in an area of van Gogh's *oeuvre* which I had been researching during the past ten years, I hesitated because of the vast and complex problems which inevitably surface when assembling well-known works within this area of nineteenth century painting. I owe him my gratitude for allowing me to realize, in exhibition form, this little-known yet important preface to modern art.

An exhibition always depends on the generosity and co-operative efforts of a great number of individuals.

In particular I should like to first express my gratitude to both participating museums, the Art Gallery of Ontario and the Rijksmuseum Vincent van Gogh, for supplying all possible physical and moral guidance. I am especially indebted to the generosity of the Van Gogh Foundation and the Director General of the Rijksmuseum Vincent van Gogh, Dr. Simon L. Levie, who have consented to the loan of 37 major works from the museum's collection, without which the representation of van Gogh's *oeuvre* would have been virtually an impossibility. William Withrow, Director of the Art Gallery of Ontario should be credited for his continual faith when moments of great financial bleakness threatened cancellation of the exhibition, and who continued to "hold the fort" and managed to make this project a reality.

My sincere appreciation to Dr. Johannes van der Wolk, Director of the Rijksmuseum Vincent van Gogh, for many organizational details in respect to his museum's collection.

Drs. Roald Nasgaard, chief curator of the Art Gallery of Ontario and Han van Crimpen, chief curator of the Rijksmuseum Vincent van Gogh, were instrumental in the negotiation of several important transatlantic loans, and I thank them both for their continual supportive co-operation and good faith.

Special thanks to the many curators from lending institutions, especially Susan Wise, Alexandra Murphy, John Walsh Jr., and Charlotta Kotik, who met my requests with such enthusiasm and professionalism.

The generosity of the many lenders to this exhibition has made this exhibition a reality. To Rudi Oxenaar, Director of the Rijksmuseum Kröller-Müller I wish to express my special gratitude for allowing six major van Gogh paintings to be reunited with other works by the Dutch artist. Gunther Busch, Director of the Bremen Kunsthalle, James Wood, Director of the Art Institute of Chicago and Robert Buck, Director of the Albright-Knox Gallery have generously lent several major works from their museums' notable collections. I wish to thank especially the many private lenders who believed in the thesis of the show and who made their paintings available for public showing.

I wish to thank the following people for their tireless efforts in their respective duties: Eva Robinson, Registrar, Barry Simpson, Exhibition Co-ordinator, Eduard Zukowski, Conservator, and Olive Koyama, Head of Publications for her patient editing and direction of the production of the catalogue. Alex MacDonald, Manager of Public Affairs, deserves credit for the energetic orchestration of what at times seemed insurmountable publication problems. Special thanks to Irene Buck for her meticulous and rapid typing of several manuscripts. To David Wistow, Education Services, my appreciation for his assistance with the preparation of catalogue entries for this publication. I am particularly indebted to Frank Newfeld for the catalogue design and production.

My final note of gratitude is extended to my mother, Slavka Ovcharov, for three years of endurance beyond the call of maternal duty and to my son, Christopher Edward, for sharing his mother with *Vincent van Gogh and the Birth of Cloisonism*.

B.W.–O.

3.
Vincent van Gogh
The Langlois Bridge with Women Washing
March 1888
oil on canvas: 54 × 65 cm
Lent by the Rijksmuseum Kröller-Müller,
Otterlo, The Netherlands

About March 17, 1888 Vincent reported to Théo that he had just completed *The Langlois Bridge*. "It is a drawbridge with a little cart going over it, outlined against a blue sky – the river blue as well, the banks orange coloured with green grass and a group of women washing linen in smocks and multicoloured caps." The very next day he wrote to Bernard for the first time from Arles, reporting enthusiastically that the countryside was as beautiful as Japan especially in "the limpidity of the atmosphere and the gay colour effects." In particular van Gogh delightedly describes to his friend how water forms patches of beautiful emerald or rich blue in the landscape. These observations can be seen as having greatly influenced his view of the Langlois Bridge, which spanned the canal from Arles to Port-de Bouc and which now has been replaced by a modern structure. The bridge motif represented for Vincent an association not only with subjects found in Japanese prints but also with the themes of similar structures from his Dutch youth. The brightly coloured dresses of the Arlesian washerwomen and the almost stained glass effect of the brilliant blue sky recalled to the artist the earlier cloisonist experiments of his friends of the "Petit Boulevard," for he wrote Théo suggesting that *The Langlois Bridge* could go to Louis Anquetin.

4.

Vincent van Gogh
The Sower
late November 1888
oil on canvas: 32 × 40 cm
Lent by the Rijksmuseum Vincent van Gogh,
Amsterdam

Throughout his life van Gogh executed drawings
and paintings of the sower, a theme owing to the
work of Millet. This one dates from the Arles
period and may be the result of praise the artist
received from Gauguin for a similar work
previously executed for the Yellow House.
Contrary to Gauguin's developing artistic theories
at the time, van Gogh purposely avoided explicit
biblical subject matter although the peasant
sowing seed has direct Christian overtones. The
landscape confirms this: the immense yellow sun
acts as a halo above the head of the toiling sower.
The painting is novel in composition. A large
dark tree-trunk thrusts diagonally across the
picture space while the figure of the peasant,
asymmetrically positioned at the left, is sharply
cropped. Van Gogh owes these design elements
to Japanese prints. The rich tonalities and heavy
contours indicate the artist's continuing concern
for the cloisonist aesthetic. His brushwork retains
its characteristic vigour.

5.

Vincent van Gogh
The Alycamps
first half November 1888
oil on canvas: 72 × 91 cm
Lent by a private collection

By the second week of November, when this
canvas was reported to Théo as being completed,
Gauguin had settled into his new lodgings with
Vincent and had judged *The Alycamps* very
much to his liking. Van Gogh produced two
versions of this site with tree trunks which "lined
like pillars along an avenue where there are rows
of old Roman tombs of a blue lilac right and
left." Two lonely figures of lovers are seen
moving through the autumnal splendour amidst
falling leaves "like snow flakes." Whether
Vincent had by this time copied Bernard's
famous canvas *Breton Women in the Meadow*
(pl. 9) which Gauguin had brought with him to
Arles remains a moot point. However, the
striking flattening of the composition and starkly
defined contour lines of the poplar trees and the
two tiny figures suggest that by late 1888 van
Gogh's understanding of Bernard's abstraction,
as presented in the exchange of series of
watercolour sketches during the summer months
(ill. 20), complemented his similar researches
into simplification of form.

10

6.
Vincent van Gogh
L'Arlésienne: Madame Ginoux with Books
November 1888
oil on canvas: 90 × 72 cm
Lent by the Metropolitan Museum of Art, New
York; Bequest of Samuel A. Lewisohn, 1951

Van Gogh completed this remarkable portrait of
Madame Ginoux, the operator of a café in Arles,
in less than one hour. The sitting took place at the
artist's studio and residence, dubbed by him
"The Yellow House," with the model positioned
in "Gauguin's armchair." The painting is an
exceptional character study of this quiet and
dignified woman of Arles, posed before some
well-thumbed volumes. Stylistically, it bears
witness to the artist's continuing belief in the
cloisonist aesthetic. Forms are simplified and
flattened; silhouettes are clearly delineated.
Colour constitutes the most powerful element of
van Gogh's artistic language. Complementary
contrasts of red-green in the book and table, and
yellow-orange-blue in the background and dress,
evoke a forcefulness of intent. Later, in St. Rémy,
van Gogh executed four more portraits of
Madame Ginoux.

7.
Vincent van Gogh
Death's-Head Moth
c. late May 1889
oil on canvas: 33 × 24 cm
Lent by the Rijksmuseum Vincent van Gogh,
Amsterdam

Van Gogh always felt a deep respect and love for
the wonders of the natural world. In a letter from
St. Rémy, where he spent much of the last year of
his life, the artist mentions the subject of this
painting, "a rather rare night moth, called the
death's-head," the name deriving from a
skull-like image visible upon the body of the
insect. Van Gogh's appreciation for the special
beauty of this delicate creature was tinged with
regret: he had to kill the moth in order to
immortalize it in paint. Perhaps he saw in his
own recent move to the St. Rémy asylum an
analogy to the fragility of life in this remarkable
being. The complex configuration of the moth's
markings make it barely distinguishable from the
rich leafy setting. Only van Gogh's use of the
complementary contrasts of red-green differ-
entiate the various forms. The canvas presents a
remarkably dynamic stylization of elements
resulting from the curvilinear outlines of
vegetation and insect alike.

Colour Plates

PLATE 1
Paul Gauguin
Undine: In the Waves
1889
oil on canvas: 92 × 72 cm
Lent by The Cleveland Museum of Art;
Gift of Mr. and Mrs. Powell Jones

This figure of Undine appeared on the
frontispiece to the Volpini exhibition catalogue,
almost certain verification of the painting's
inclusion in the famous show. The work was
probably executed in Brittany in early spring
1889 or else shortly after Gauguin's return to
Paris. He undoubtedly completed the canvas in
part from memory, since no model could pose in
such a setting. The nude's awkward position,
viewed from the rear, is indebted to Degas and
Japanese prints as is her asymmetrical placement
in the composition. The precise contour lines and
vivid tonalities result in one of Gauguin's finest
cloisonist works. The subject of the painting, the
sea nymph Undine, may have symbolized for the
artist the renewal of life, her watery realm
commonly being associated with childbirth. Not
just Undine's but all womanly powers of
procreation have been evoked by Gauguin in this
mysterious painting.

PLATE 2
Louis Anquetin
Avenue de Clichy: Five O'Clock in the Evening
1887
oil on canvas: 69.2 × 53 cm
Lent by the Wadsworth Atheneum, Hartford,
Connecticut; Ella Gallup Sumner and Mary
Catlin Sumner Collection

At his parent's home in Normandy, Anquetin discovered that as he looked through the variously coloured window panes of his father's front door, each pane influenced differently the psychological mood of the landscape he perceived. The experiment, according to Bernard, was illustrated by Anquetin in two paintings: *The Mower* (pl. 4) and *Avenue de Clichy*. Here the artist has depicted city life at twilight on the popular Avenue de Clichy in Montmartre. The special ambience is conveyed by the predominantly blue monochrome tonality and complementary contrasts of yellow-orange. The critic Edouard Dujardin was first to label this painting's use of flat areas of pure colour and heavy outline "cloisonism:" a reference to medieval cloisonné enamel work and gothic stained-glass windows.

PLATE 3
Vincent van Gogh
The Café Terrace on the Place du Forum, Arles at Night
September 1888
oil on canvas: 81 × 65.5 cm
Lent by the Rijksmuseum Kröller-Müller, Otterlo, The Netherlands

This painting reveals a debt to Louis Anquetin's canvas, *Avenue de Clichy: Five O'Clock in the Evening* (pl. 2). Van Gogh was fascinated at the time by night scenes which included effects of artificial and natural illumination. Here a gas-jet blazes brightly on the terrace of the café while stars glow in the evening sky. To execute the work on location van Gogh devised an elaborate hat fixed with candles.

PLATE 4
Louis Anquetin
The Mower at Noon: Summer
1887
oil on cardboard (carton): 69.2 × 52.7 cm
Lent by Prof. and Madame Léon Velluz, Paris

Along with the *Avenue de Clichy* (pl. 2), the *Mower* serves as a unique surviving witness to Anquetin's role in the inception of cloisonism in 1887. The canvas depicts harvest time, painted in warm tones of yellow-orange-red as if perceived through a yellow pane of glass. Van Gogh indicated that Anquetin's *Mower* expressed nature admirably according to the naive images of the land found in popular country almanacs. The high horizoned composition and simplified, flattened forms can thus be seen as indebted to the above source as well as to Japanese prints.

PLATE 5
Vincent van Gogh
The Mowers, Arles in the Background
1888
oil on canvas: 73 × 54 cm
Lent by the Musée Rodin, Paris

On June 28, 1888 Vincent wrote his close friend Emile Bernard of his deep admiration of Anquetin's *The Mower at Noon* (pl. 4) which he had seen in Paris. In particular he was struck by the latter's new simplified style which rendered the setting of a sunny countryside during harvest time "in a wholly primitive manner" like those naive images to be found in popular country almanacs. In August, van Gogh attempted to capture the essence of harvest time in Arles in his *Mower* by using a similar predominant yellow monochrome colour scheme and simplified composition closely related to Anquetin's *The Mower*.

PLATE 6
Emile Bernard
Still Life with Blue Coffeepot
1888
oil on canvas: 55 × 46 cm
Lent by the Kunsthalle, Bremen

Several still life paintings by Bernard which appear to have been executed by the winter of 1887-88 support Bernard's claim that both he and Anquetin were researching the problems of simplification and abstraction during these years in Paris. The *Blue Coffeepot* is a striking example of such colour and linear investigations undertaken by Bernard before his journey in summer 1888 and work with Paul Gauguin in Pont-Aven. Although dated 1888, van Gogh had seen it in an unfinished state while in Paris, and it appears to have influenced a still life with similar motifs by van Gogh, executed in Arles.

PLATE 7
Paul Gauguin
The Vision after the Sermon
1888
oil on canvas: 73 × 92 cm
National Gallery of Scotland, Edinburgh (not in exhibition)

Although this painting was not available for the exhibition, it represents the first synthetist manifestation in Gauguin's *oeuvre* by summer 1888. Bernard documented later that Gauguin was impressed by the distinctive simplification of the younger artist's earlier *Breton Women in the Meadow* (pl. 9), and thus was impelled to

respond to the young artist's innovative ideas by producing *The Vision*. Gauguin's belief that "art is an abstraction [derived]...from nature" is forcefully presented in this image. The biblical story of Jacob wrestling with the Angel takes place in a Breton landscape, a vision experienced by the local peasantry after a Sunday sermon. "To me in this painting," Gauguin wrote, "the landscape and the struggle exist only in the imagination of these praying people." The distorted perspective, flattened forms and flaming colouration of the background indicate Gauguin's evolving anti-naturalism.

PLATE 8
Emile Bernard
The Buckwheat Harvesters: Le Blé noir
1888
oil on canvas: 72 × 92 cm
Lent by a private collection, Switzerland

Le Blé noir dates from autumn of 1888 when Bernard was working on the Brittany coast, in company with Gauguin. Scenes of local Breton peasant life were prevalent in both these artists' canvases at the time. Bernard's stylized portrayal of buckwheat harvesting employs typical cloisonist design elements – flat patterning, dark contour lines and ambiguous spatial recession. Striking red-orange tonalities pervade the image, indicating the close stylistic relationships between Bernard's canvas and Gauguin's contemporaneous *Vision after the Sermon* (pl. 7).

PLATE 9
Emile Bernard
Breton Women in the Meadow: Pardon at Pont-Aven
1888
oil on canvas: 74 × 92 cm
Lent by a private collection, Paris

Controversy still rages as to whether this painting, executed in Brittany after Bernard's arrival in Pont-Aven *circa* September 1888, influenced the creation of Gauguin's masterpiece, *The Vision after the Sermon* (pl. 7). Certainly, Bernard's cloisonist tendencies here – the absence of spatial recession, the truncated figures and unmodelled colours – undoubtedly affected Gauguin's major canvas and his subsequent style. *The Vision*, however, employs these design elements to convey a profound spirituality which has been questioned in the present work. Although Bernard was steeped in Breton Catholicism, it was only by 1892 he entitled this painting *Pardon at Pont-Aven*.

PLATE 10
Vincent van Gogh
Breton Women in the Meadow [after Emile Bernard]
October-December 1888
watercolour on cardboard: 47.5 × 62 cm
Lent by the Galleria Civica d'Arte Moderna, Milan

This study is a copy by van Gogh after Bernard's controversial oil painting of identical title. Gauguin had brought the canvas from Pont-Aven to Arles in October 1888. Vincent was particularly appreciative of Bernard's vigorous treatment and the pure naivete of the ensemble. Although the Dutchman failed to repeat the arbitrary tonalities of the Breton costumes and green background of Bernard's painting, several other features of the original have been maintained, such as the basic composition, the strong outlining and large areas of unmodelled colour.

PLATE 11
Vincent van Gogh
Portrait of Père Tanguy
late 1887
oil on canvas: 65 × 51 cm
Lent by a private collection

Julien François Tanguy was born in Brittany and first practised the profession of plasterer. By 1865 he was in Paris, employed as a colour salesman, and soon thereafter he became a staunch supporter of Impressionism. Around 1873 he opened a little paint and art supply shop which was frequented by such avant-garde artists as Pissarro, Renoir, Gauguin, van Gogh, Bernard, Anquetin and Lautrec. Tanguy's warm humanity appealed strongly to van Gogh who executed at least three portraits of him. Here the dealer sits positioned frontally with hands clasped, surrounded by a rich display of Japanese prints whose aesthetic so profoundly influenced French art of the period.

PLATE 12
Vincent van Gogh
The Italian Woman with Daisies: La Segatori
late 1887
oil on canvas: 81 × 60 cm
Lent by the Musée d'Orsay, Paris

Painted shortly before van Gogh left Paris for Arles in February 1888, this portrait may represent Agostina Segatori, the owner of the café *Le Tambourin*. She and van Gogh had had a brief relationship. Dressed in regional costume and holding two flowers, La Segatori undoubtedly expressed for van Gogh an archetypal image of womanhood. The painting's flattened background, sharply silhouetted forms and vibrant colouration are evidence of the artist's concern for characteristic cloisonist effects.

PLATE 13
Vincent van Gogh
Interior of a Restaurant
summer 1887
oil on canvas: 45.5 × 56.5 cm
Lent by the Rijksmuseum Kröller-Müller, Otterlo, The Netherlands

By mid summer 1887 van Gogh was working extensively in the environs of the Parisian suburbs of Asnières. This restaurant interior probably represents one of van Gogh's dining places there. The subject is treated with a quasi-pointillist technique which expresses the artist's awareness of the neo-Impressionist style, specifically the colour theory of Seurat. Van Gogh has juxtaposed small dabs of pure colour–frequently complementaries, as visible on the red-green wall. Passages, however, such as the chairs indicate how easily the artist returned to a characteristic realism.

PLATE 14
Vincent van Gogh
Vincent's House on the Place Lamartine, Arles
late September 1888
oil on canvas: 76 × 94 cm
Lent by the Rijksmuseum Vincent van Gogh, Amsterdam

Van Gogh leased this corner property in Arles as his intended "studio of the south" and spent considerable time and money furnishing it. Of his artist friends, only Gauguin utilized the rent-free facilities of the so-called Yellow House. Van Gogh wrote that the building as subject matter was "frightfully difficult; but that is just why I want to conquer it. It's terrific, these houses, yellow in the sun, and the incomparable freshness of the blue."

PLATE 15
Vincent van Gogh
Vincent's Bedroom at Arles
October 1888
oil on canvas: 56.5 × 74 cm
Lent by the Rijksmuseum Vincent van Gogh, Amsterdam

In October 1888 van Gogh painted this famous view of his bedroom in the Yellow House. On the walls hang several of his canvases including two identifiable portraits and a landscape. "Here colour is to do everything," van Gogh wrote of the work, "and giving by its simplification a grander style to things, is to be suggestive here of *rest* or of sleep in general. . . . The shadows and the cast shadows are suppressed; it is painted in free tints like the Japanese prints."

PLATE 16
Jakob Meyer de Haan
Breton Women Scutching Hemp
1889
fresco (transferred wall mural): 133.7 × 202 cm
Lent by an anonymous collection, San Diego

One of the purest examples of the cloisonist style within the group of artists of the Pont-Aven school is this large fresco mural by the Dutch artist Meyer de Haan, executed for the small dining room of the Inn of Marie Henry on the desolate Breton coast in the village of Le Pouldu. Two starkly simplified figures of Breton women in their Le Pouldu costumes are represented stretching or "scutching" hemp. On the same wall next to this mural, Gauguin painted his fresco *Joan of Arc* (pl. 17) in a complementary highly synthetist style and a theme repetitive of the hardships of life and labour in Brittany. De Haan's mural remained hidden and forgotten until in 1924 a local craftsman redecorating the inn discovered these frescoes under several layers of wallpaper.

PLATE 17
Paul Gauguin
Joan of Arc
1889
fresco (transferred wall mural): 116 × 58 cm
Anonymous loan

As in his famous *Breton Calvary: The Green Christ* (pl. 23) the *Joan of Arc* is to be seen as a narrative, representing the Breton soul, its costumes and landscape. A young barefooted girl from Le Pouldu is perhaps here identified by the artist with the universal image of the poor "Maid of Orleans," Joan of Arc. Her simplified sorrowful features and plain Breton costume are set against a barren coastal view populated by a single cow and the tiny figure of a labourer on the left in the distance. Vibrant blues and oranges animate the setting in contrast, as Gauguin wrote, to "the poverty in life" of the Breton people. Both *Joan of Arc* and *Scutching Hemp* (pl. 16) were executed side by side in the wall of the dining room of the Inn of Marie Henry and illustrate the high degree of cloisonist/synthetist style that had been evolved by Gauguin and Meyer de Haan by 1889.

PLATE 18
Vincent van Gogh
Still Life: Vase with Fourteen Sunflowers
January 1889
oil on canvas: 95 × 73 cm
Lent by the Rijksmuseum Vincent van Gogh, Amsterdam

During his stay in Paris, van Gogh's passion for the sunflower motif had already surfaced in several canvases. But it was only upon his arrival in Arles and with the renting of his Yellow House (pl. 14) that he revealed to Bernard his plan to decorate his studio "with a half a dozen pictures of sunflowers" whose "raw or broken chrome yellows will blaze forth in various backgrounds." Significantly he saw these vibrant sunflowers as capable of producing coloured effects like those of "stained glass windows in a Gothic church." The Dutch artist conceived the *Still Life with Fourteen Sunflowers* not only as a highly cloisonist image; he also considered the colour yellow as symbolic of gratitude and producing a sense of comfort.

PLATE 20
Still Life: Vase with Fourteen Sunflowers
1888
oil on canvas: 93 × 73 cm
National Gallery, London;
Courtauld Fund [not in exhibition]

PLATE 19
Vincent van Gogh
La Berceuse: Madame Augustine Roulin
1889
oil on canvas: 92 × 72 cm
Lent by the Museum of Fine Arts, Boston;
Bequest of John T. Spaulding

The family of the postman Joseph Roulin provided van Gogh in Arles with warm familial attention and much needed psychological security. The artist seems to have associated Madame Roulin with the universal image of motherhood. He depicts her here as holding a rope about to rock the cradle, in order to provide mankind with consoling solace. Her green dress and orange hair set against a green background with pink dahlias produced, according to him, a discordant note. Such strident colouration was likened by the artist to cheap coloured popular prints of the nineteenth century. Significantly van Gogh saw the *Berceuse* as a modern madonna of the common people, to be flanked on either side by a canvas of flaming yellow sunflowers (pls. 18 and 20) which were to act as torches or candelabras.

PLATE 21
Paul Gauguin
The Breton Calvary: The Green Christ
c. October-November 1889
oil on canvas: 92 × 73 cm
Lent by the Musées Royaux des Beaux-Arts de Belgique, Brussels

A moss-covered Pièta at the village of Nizon near Pont-Aven on the Brittany coast provided the source for this painting, hence its title. Christ's suffering on the cross is clearly identified with the hard life of the Breton peasant and the personal miseries Gauguin experienced at this time. The artist may well have seen himself as the "passive lamb" (a reference to the martyred Christ) visible beside the Breton woman at the lower right. Gauguin sought to express human hardship and not to relieve it, as was the case with van Gogh.

PLATE 22
Paul Gauguin
The Yellow Christ
1889
oil on canvas: 92 × 73 cm
Lent by the Albright-Knox Gallery, Buffalo;
General Purchase Fund

Based on an actual polychromed (yellow) wood sculpture in a chapel near Pont-Aven, this wayside crucifix conveys, in Gauguin's own words, the "great rustic and superstitious simplicity" of the Breton peasantry. The painting presents a visual metaphor of their deep-rooted faith. The flat, linear treatment of the praying women, the Christ on the cross and the vivid landscape behind result in one of Gauguin's most powerful religious images. He later included the work in a self-portrait to express the Christ-like suffering of all artists.

PLATE 23
Paul Gauguin
Grape Gathering–Human Misery: Vendages à Arles–Misères Humaines
1889
oil on canvas: 73.5 × 92.5 cm
Lent by the Ordrupgaardsamlingen, Copenhagen; Collection of William Hansen

This is one of Gauguin's numerous memory-paintings, an approach strongly advocated by the artist. Executed in Arles in fall 1888, the work depicts an Arlesian grape harvest but with Breton peasant women. "So much the worse for exactitude," as Gauguin put it. He went on to describe the painting as "done with bold outlines enclosing tones which are almost uniform and laid on very thickly with a palette knife." Gauguin makes no mention of the melancholic figure in the foreground whose presence undoubtedly suggested the title of this remarkable work.

PLATE 24
Paul Gauguin
Women at Arles: The Mistral
1888
oil on canvas: 73 × 92 cm
Lent by the Art Institute of Chicago;
Mr. and Mrs. L.L. Coburn Memorial Collection

The setting of this important work is the public park at Arles, opposite the Yellow House where Gauguin stayed for two months with van Gogh in 1888. The curving path, brightly hued picket-gate and conical cypresses wrapped in burlap are all identifiable. The women, dressed in typical Arlesienne costume, shiver in the cold air of the fall Mistral. The precise meaning of the work is unknown. Recently references have been made to Gauguin's inclusion of a self-portrait in the bush at the lower left.

PLATE 25
Emile Bernard
Afternoon at St. Briac
1887
oil on canvas: 48 × 54 cm
Lent by the Aargauer Kunsthaus, Aarau, Switzerland

In the summer of 1887 Bernard travelled to the coastal village of St. Briac in Brittany and settled there for two months to paint vibrant and highly simplified landscapes of the region. This view of the bay at St. Briac represents a unique example of the advanced cloisonist style created by the nineteen-year-old artist. Two years later he chose to exhibit this and another painting under his pseudonym "Nemo" along with twenty-two other works at the café Volpini in Paris with the "Groupe Impressioniste et Synthetiste."

PLATE 26
Emile Bernard
The Ragpickers at Asnières (Clichy)
late autumn, 1887
oil on canvas: 45.9 × 54.2 cm
Lent by the Museum of Modern Art, New York;
Grace Rainy Rogers Fund, 1962

Both van Gogh and Bernard painted views of the railway bridge at Clichy in Asnières, a suburb of Paris where the latter's parents lived. Bernard's vision stresses the interplay of straight and curved lines together with large areas of unmodelled colour suggestive of Japanist influences. Bernard was also indebted to the diagonally structured compositions in the works of Signac and Seurat. This painting of 1887, in its marked simplification of forms (such as the two ragpickers), permits Bernard rightfully to claim a collaborative role with Anquetin in the inception of cloisonism.

PLATE 27
Louis Anquetin
The Bridge of Saintes-Pères: Gust of Wind
c.1889
oil on canvas: 119.5 × 126 cm
Lent by the Kunsthalle, Bremen

By 1889 Anquetin's bold simplified style was clearly established in such decorative canvases as the *Gust of Wind*. The stark, dark outlines of his earlier *Avenue de Clichy* (pl. 2) have here been replaced by a highly expressive and mannered line which can be seen as anticipating the Art Nouveau style of the next decade. Anquetin's notorious penchant for depicting contemporary life in Paris is here intermingled with his almost obsessive admiration and powerful anatomical understanding of horses. The bridges of Paris appear frequently in many Impressionist paintings; both Bernard and van Gogh favoured similar views of Parisian architectural landmarks in the outskirts of Montmartre as exemplified in Bernard's *The Ragpickers at Asnières (Clichy)* (pl. 28).

PLATE 28
Henri de Toulouse-Lautrec
At the Circus Fernando
1887
oil on canvas: 100.3 × 161.3 cm
Lent by the Art Institute of Chicago;
the Joseph Winterbotham Collection

Toulouse-Lautrec executed many fine studies of Parisian circuses. This large scale work depicts the *Cirque Fernando* in Montmartre, a favourite haunt of the artist. Monsieur Loyal, its well-known ring-master, is visible at the left. His truncated figure juxtaposed against the unmodelled, shadowless floor suggests the influence of both Degas and Japanese prints. The painting was purchased by the directors of the *Moulin Rouge* and hung in its entrance hall.

PLATE 29
Henri de Toulouse-Lautrec
The Ball at the Moulin de la Galette
1889
oil on canvas: 90 × 100 cm
Lent by the Art Institute of Chicago;
Mr. and Mrs. E.L. Coburn Memorial Collection

Until the *Moulin Rouge* dance hall opened in late 1889, Lautrec was a constant frequenter of this one-time mill turned into a dance hall on the hill of Montmartre. It was an especially popular place, where on Sunday workers, painters and models went to dance. Here Lautrec depicts the artist and later owner of this painting, Joseph Albert, sitting in the right foreground intently engrossed by the motley array of bohemian and working class dancers. The raking diagonal of the bench back and floor boards displays Lautrec's deep fascination with Japanese prints and personal approach to problems of simplification within the group of the "Petit Boulevard" artists.

PLATE 30
Louis Anquetin
The Dance Hall at the Moulin Rouge
c.1893
oil on canvas: 169 × 205 cm
Lent by a private collection, Switzerland

Anquetin's youthful friendship and close artistic relationship with Toulouse-Lautrec is best summed up in this painting executed by late 1893. The two artists were assiduous frequenters of the *Moulin Rouge* dance hall in Montmartre. During the years 1888 and 1890 Lautrec and Anquetin experimented with intense pure flat colour juxtapositions and formal simplifications, and avidly studied Japanese prints. These researches led both artists to execute several canvases depicting bohemian night life. *At the Moulin Rouge* can be seen to represent both a "swan song" to Anquetin's earlier cloisonist style and a tribute to Lautrec's famous dance hall canvases such as the *Moulin de la Galette* (pl. 31). Anquetin boldly copied the dancing figure of Jane Avril from Lautrec's famous poster (1893) and placed her as a focal point in his dance hall interior.

PLATE 31
Paul Gauguin
Still Life Fête Gloanec
1888
oil on wood panel: 38 × 53 cm
Lent by the Musée des Beaux-Arts d'Orléans, Orléans, France

Gauguin painted many still lifes during his career, this one dating from summer 1888 at Pont-Aven. The canvas was exhibited at the name-day celebrations of his pension manageress, Mlle Marie Jeanne Gloanec. More conservative artist-lodgers had forbidden Gauguin to hang any work during the festivities and so he was obliged to sign the name of Bernard's sister, Madeleine. Few would have been deceived. The unusual vantage point, the simplified contours of objects, and the glowing tones of the table top are characteristic of Gauguin's bold approach at the time.

PLATE 32
Charles Laval
Going to the Market
1888
oil on canvas: 36 × 46 cm
Lent by a private collection, Switzerland

Laval was a close follower of Gauguin. Together they travelled to Panama and Martinique and worked in Brittany during the summer of 1888. This canvas, later to be displayed at the famous Volpini show, dates from shortly after Bernard's arrival at Pont-Aven in August of that year. His influence is evident in the painting's brilliant colour patterns and confusing spatial organization.

PLATE 1
Paul Gauguin
Undine: In the Waves
1889
oil on canvas: 92 × 72 cm

PLATE 2
Louis Anquetin
Avenue de Clichy: Five O'Clock in the Evening
1887
oil on canvas: 69.2 × 53 cm

PLATE 3
Vincent van Gogh
The Café Terrace on the Place du Forum, Arles at Night
September 1888
oil on canvas: 81 × 65.5 cm

PLATE 4
Louis Anquetin
The Mower at Noon: Summer
1887
oil on cardboard (carton): 69.2 × 52.7 cm

PLATE 5
Vincent van Gogh
The Mowers, Arles in the Background
1888
oil on canvas: 73 × 54 cm

PLATE 6
Emile Bernard
Still Life with Blue Coffeepot
1888
oil on canvas: 55 × 46 cm

PLATE 7
Paul Gauguin
The Vision after the Sermon
1888
oil on canvas: 73 × 92 cm

PLATE 8
Emile Bernard
The Buckwheat Harvesters: Le Blé noir
1888
oil on canvas: 72 × 92 cm

PLATE 9
Emile Bernard
Breton Women in the Meadow: Pardon at Pont-Aven
1888
oil on canvas: 74 × 92 cm

PLATE 10
Vincent van Gogh
Breton Women in the Meadow [after Emile Bernard]
October-December 1888
watercolour on cardboard: 47.5 × 62 cm

23

PLATE 11
Vincent van Gogh
Portrait of Père Tanguy
late 1887
oil on canvas: 65 × 51 cm

PLATE 12
Vincent van Gogh
The Italian Woman with Daisies: La Segatori
late 1887
oil on canvas: 81 × 60 cm

PLATE 13
Vincent van Gogh
Interior of a Restaurant
summer 1887
oil on canvas: 45.5 × 56.5 cm

PLATE 14
Vincent van Gogh
Vincent's House on the Place Lamartine, Arles
late September 1888
oil on canvas: 76 × 94 cm

PLATE 15
Vincent van Gogh
Vincent's Bedroom at Arles
October 1888
oil on canvas: 56.5 × 74 cm

PLATE 16
Jakob Meyer de Haan
Breton Women Scutching Hemp
1889
fresco (transferred wall mural): 133.7 × 202 cm

PLATE 17
Paul Gauguin
Joan of Arc
1889
fresco (transferred wall mural): 116 × 58 cm

PLATE 18
Vincent van Gogh
Still Life: Vase with Fourteen Sunflowers
January 1889
oil on canvas: 95 × 73 cm

PLATE 19
Vincent van Gogh
La Berceuse: Madame Augustine Roulin
1889
oil on canvas: 92 × 72 cm

PLATE 20
Vincent van Gogh
Still Life: Vase with Fourteen Sunflowers
1888
oil on canvas: 93 × 73 cm

PLATE 21
Paul Gauguin
The Breton Calvary: The Green Christ
c. October-November 1889
oil on canvas: 92 × 73 cm

PLATE 22
Paul Gauguin
The Yellow Christ
1889
oil on canvas: 92 × 73 cm

PLATE 23
Paul Gauguin
Grape Gathering–Human Misery: Vendages à
Arles–Misères Humaines
1889
oil on canvas: 73.5 × 92.5 cm

PLATE 24
Paul Gauguin
Women at Arles: The Mistral
1888
oil on canvas: 73 × 92 cm

PLATE 25
Emile Bernard
Afternoon at St. Briac
1887
oil on canvas: 48 × 54 cm

PLATE 26
Emile Bernard
The Ragpickers at Asnières (Clichy)
late autumn, 1887
oil on canvas: 45.9 × 54.2 cm

PLATE 28
Henri de Toulouse-Lautrec
At the Circus Fernando
1887
oil on canvas: 100.3 × 161.3 cm

PLATE 27
Louis Anquetin
The Bridge of Saintes-Pères: Gust of Wind
c.1889
oil on canvas: 119.5 × 126 cm

PLATE 29
Henri de Toulouse-Lautrec
The Ball at the Moulin de la Galette
1889
oil on canvas: 90 × 100 cm

PLATE 30
Louis Anquetin
The Dance Hall at the Moulin Rouge
c.1893
oil on canvas: 169 × 205 cm

PLATE 31
Paul Gauguin
Still Life Fête Gloanec
1888
oil on wood panel: 38 × 53 cm

PLATE 32
Charles Laval
Going to the Market
1888
oil on canvas: 36 × 46 cm

Vincent van Gogh and the Birth of Cloisonism

It remains uncertain whether Vincent van Gogh is best known for his art or for his self-mutilation of an ear and eventual suicide. The popularization of Vincent as a mad genius has created the impression that his work blossomed in isolation from other artists and cultural tradition. Yet even the greatest artists are a phenomenon of their own times, and Vincent was no exception.

Although Dutch by birth, Vincent worked in France from 1886 until his death and trained himself to see things with "an eye more Japanese," as he once said in reference to the oriental woodblock prints he so dearly loved. While still in The Netherlands, he considered himself an heir of the French Realist painter J.F. Millet. After his arrival in Paris he not only studied and worked in the manner of the Impressionists, the Neo-Impressionists (Pointillists) and the Japanese coloured print, but also gradually built up a circle of friends and acquaintances among the younger *avant-garde* artists, which included such men as Louis Anquetin, Emile Bernard, Henri de Toulouse-Lautrec, Paul Signac and eventually Paul Gauguin and Georges Seurat.

The principal aim of the present exhibition is to examine Vincent van Gogh's personal development in the light of his evolving relationships with the art of a number of his closest French colleagues. The exhibition title *Vincent van Gogh and the Birth of Cloisonism* refers directly to one of these relationships; namely, to a style of painting evolved by late 1887 by Vincent's fellow painter Louis Anquetin.

Anquetin had been, with Toulouse-Lautrec and Emile Bernard, a student at the art school of Fernand Cormon, where Vincent also came to study. By the end of 1886 all four students had rebelled against the academic precepts taught at such art schools as this and were painting in a more or less Impressionist manner, flirting with either Pointillist style or the scientific laws of colour contrast upon which this style was known to be based. Anquetin quickly decided against the stipple technique of Pointillism and in several major works, especially *Avenue de Clichy: Five O'Clock in the Evening* (pl. 2) and *The Mower at Noon* (pl. 4) worked in a style which early the following year was named Cloisonism, likely with his knowledge and support, by the French symbolist writer and critic Edouard Dujardin.

8.
Vincent van Gogh
Window of Vincent's Studio at Saint Paul's Hospital
May-early June 1889
Black chalk, gouache on paper: 61.5 × 47 cm
Lent by the Rijksmuseum Vincent van Gogh, Amsterdam

After a brief stay in the hospital at Arles following his first attack, Vincent wrote on May 8, 1889 to Théo expressing his contentment for having voluntarily incarcerated himself in Saint Paul's Hospital at St. Rémy where, he reports, he finds himself surrounded by the "reality of life of the various madmen and lunatics in this menagerie." Two weeks later he announces that he has been given a little room with greenish-gray wallpaper and with curtains and, because there are more than thirty empty rooms, he has also been given an extra room to work in. This gouache represents this new studio, its curtainless stark simplicity decorated by Vincent's supplies on the ledge and on the table, lower right, and by his recent works, hanging on the walls. The interior remains a testimony to van Gogh's continued faith despite moments of despair and a symbol of the recuperative powers of artistic creativity. Two other views of the interior of the asylum – a corridor and the vestibule of the hospital – were executed during the same time as *The Window* in a similar bold linear style. However his previous brilliant colour experiments in Arles are gradually being replaced by such earthy tones as red ochre and raw sienna reminiscent of van Gogh's earlier Dutch palette.

9.
Vincent van Gogh
View at Auvers
June-July 1890
oil on canvas: 50 × 52 cm
Lent by the Rijksmuseum Vincent van Gogh,
Amsterdam

"Auvers is very beautiful, among other things a
lot of old thatched roofs which are getting rare . . .
it is the real country and picturesque." So van
Gogh described his first happy impressions of his
new surroundings to Théo and his young wife on
May 20. In this canvas Vincent expresses his
tranquil first few days at Auvers, a village on the
river Oise. He portrays the "lush well kept
greenery" and quiet surroundings of Auvers'
cottages and middle-class dwellings, while
retaining the simplicity and defined cloisonist
lines of his Arles-St. Rémy periods. In recent
months Vincent had confessed a nostalgic
yearning to see his native land again and perhaps
in Auvers such desires were being reawakened.
He suggested to Théo that he saw in the
landscapes of Auvers a "quiet like a Puvis de
Chavannes, no factories," only verdant abun-
dance, but he must also have been aware of such
panoramic views of Auvers as painted earlier by
Cézanne and Pissarro. In the last days before his
suicide on July 29, his increasing nervous
intensity precluded similar bucolic and tranquil
views and he produced large threatening
canvases of fields of wheat which he wrote are
placed "under troubled skies, and I did not need
to go out of my way to try to express sadness and
extreme loneliness."

The name Cloisonism was derived from a designation for a type of inlaid enamel work
which had been widely used in Byzantine and related Western Medieval forms of religious
art. The chief characteristics of this style were fields of flat, bright colouration separated
into compartments by outline contours of wire or ridges left by gouging a metal plate. The
result was analogous to stained glass windows and other forms of medieval art featuring
intense colours, strong figural outlines and little, if any, modelling in the round. In
nineteenth century France this so-called *cloisonné* enamel work was often associated with
the similarly bold outlines and bright colours of enamelled or porcelain vases, particularly
those of Oriental manufacture or derivations thereof. Dujardin's article on Anquetin drew
a further analogy with the inexpensive medievalizing coloured woodblock prints known in
France as Images from Epinal, which was one centre of production. This implies the idea
shared within our chosen circle of artists that naive or primitive art forms provided a better
model for modern artists, because more true to basic human instincts, than the artificial art
of the fashionable salons, where elaborate historical and mythological allegories were still
seen as the highest form of painting.

Vincent had left Paris in February 1888 in order to work at Arles in southern France,
to experience the brighter sunlight in what he considered both the Mediterranean terrain of
his hero Eugène Delacroix and the place in the west where Japanese artists would feel most
at home. He also hoped to found there a "studio of the south," a haven for like-minded
artists who wished to escape the debilitating effects of urban life in the French capital. Here
Vincent wished to reunite what he called the "Impressionists of the Little Boulevard," the
circle of younger Impressionists mentioned above, who had not yet achieved enough
success to warrant support by the fashionable art dealers with shops located on the "great
boulevards" near the Paris Opera house. Vincent had already organized displays of
Japanese prints, of his own work and that of the group of friends which included
Anquetin, Bernard and Lautrec on the walls of Paris restaurants. From the south he was
not adverse to repeating this experience, even after he and his colleagues had begun to send
submissions to various exhibition societies in Paris and Brussels.

Even the typically unenvious Vincent was slightly taken back to learn that Dujardin
had singled out Anquetin as the leader of a new anti-Pointillist tendency in French
painting. He maintained to his brother, Théo (a leading Parisian dealer in Impressionist
art) that Georges Seurat, the founder of the Neo-Impressionist school, still deserved to be
called the leader of the new tendency, and that Bernard had gone further than Anquetin in
what he termed the Japanese manner. This momentary expression of pique notwithstand-
ing, Vincent produced in 1888 a number of variations on Anquetin's *Mower* (see pl. 5).
His justly famous *The Café Terrace: Arles at Night* (pl. 3) is now also considered a tribute
to Anquetin's *Avenue de Clichy*.

During the summer of 1888 Gauguin, Bernard and Charles Laval worked together at the picturesque village of Pont-Aven in Brittany and produced such pristine examples of the Cloisonist style as Gauguin's *Still Life Fête Gloanec* (pl. 21), Bernard's *Breton Women in the Meadow* (pl. 9) and Laval's *Going to the Market* (pl. 22). These stylistic innovations are best known as the Pont-Aven school or Synthetism (that is, a synthetic treatment of line and colour), but it is significant that both Bernard and the Nabi artist Maurice Denis characterized Synthetism as a stage between Cloisonism and Symbolism in the development of the latter movement in painting. Debating terminology and arguing the almost hopeless question of who got there first naturally confuses the question of appropriate labels for specific movements and groupings. Let us agree that in French painting of the late 1880s the ideas lying behind Cloisonism, Synthetism and Symbolism involve intentional ambiguity among elements of style, subject choice and ultimate meaning which it may prove impossible to unravel. This apparent confusion between stylistic and iconographic elements (that is, what a particular gesture, symbol or colour "means") is a result of the gradual accumulation of associated meanings of the figural, landscape and still life subjects preferred by the several artists under consideration.

At one point in the summer of 1888, Bernard, Gauguin and Laval planned to visit and work with Vincent at the "yellow house" which he had rented in anticipation of some such visit, but only Gauguin came to Arles in late October. The tragic outcome of this association – with Vincent's breakdown and subsequent voluntary committal to the Hospital at St. Rémy – is well known. Less known to the general public are the intensely creative exchanges between Gauguin and van Gogh and also with Bernard, Anquetin, Laval and Lautrec, which accompanied these changing personal relationships. These relationships involved a striking variety of friendships, correspondence and joint exhibitions which is virtually unique in the history of Western painting, at least in reference to the significance – major or minor – of the artists concerned.

Following the crisis between van Gogh and Gauguin in Arles, one might easily imagine that all dreams of fraternal association were ended. Not so. Vincent continued to correspond with Gauguin, who received further support from Théo, and Vincent's participation at the famous Volpini exhibition at the Paris World Fair of 1889 was prevented not by Gauguin but rather by Théo's feeling that this would be entering the event "by the back stairs." In short, the record of apparent dispute and hurt feelings should not be thought to prove a case of irreconcilable differences. Personal differences aside, all these important figures within the movement that eventually was to be known as Post-Impressionism are to be considered fellow travellers in the same artistic direction.

10.
Paul Gauguin (1848-1903)
Still Life with Profile of Laval
late (?) 1886
oil on canvas: 46 × 38 cm
Lent by a private collection, Switzerland

This painting may have been executed after Gauguin's return to Paris from Brittany in 1886. The centrally positioned still-life, including a curious ceramic sculpture by Gauguin, suggests the influence of Cézanne, even to its colouration and brushwork. To the right is partially visible the head of Gauguin's friend, Charles Laval, with whom he travelled to Panama and Martinique the following year. Seen in profile, Laval's image is dramatically cropped and asymmetrically positioned, doubtless evidence of Degas' influence. He and Gauguin had renewed their acquaintance at this time after a previous falling-out. Laval's unusual proximity to the still-life and his closed eyes create a sense of mystery and ambiguity in the work which to date remains inexplicable.

11.
Paul Gauguin
Among the Mangoes: Martinique
c. late July-early August 1887
oil on canvas: 89 × 116 cm
Lent by the Rijksmuseum Vincent van Gogh,
Amsterdam

Gauguin left Paris for Panama on April 10, 1887 with his friend Charles Laval. After a brief stay there, they journeyed to the island of Martinique where for the first time Gauguin painted the exotic colours and subject matter of tropical climes. The idyllic existence of the natives fascinated him. "What agrees with me most are the human figures which each day come and go attired with coloured finery and moving with an infinitely varied grace. At present I restrain myself to making sketch after sketch with the aim of penetrating their character until finally I shall have them pose. Even while carrying heavy loads on their heads they chatter away without stopping. Their gestures are very special and their hands play a great role in harmony with balancing the hips." Gauguin returned to France in November suffering from acute dysentery. His painting received less than enthusiastic reviews and was labelled 'barbaric' and 'troublesome.' However the voyage to Martinique had not been in vain. Gauguin had tasted the luxuriant atmosphere of the south which no doubt prompted his later sojourns in Tahiti.

12.
Paul Gauguin
Self Portrait: "Les Misérables" dedicated to his friend Vincent
1888
oil on canvas: 45 × 55 cm
Lent by the Rijksmuseum Vincent van Gogh, Amsterdam

The important and unique exchange of self portraits among Gauguin, Bernard (ill. 18) and Laval (ill. 27) was instigated by van Gogh in Arles around mid September 1888. Consistent with his goal to some day see a fraternal community of modern artists in the South of France, perhaps in his little "Yellow House" (pl. 14), he told Bernard his idea of the creation of portraits among his fellow artists in Pont-Aven. He explained that Japanese artists who also lived and worked together in harmony very often exchanged works among themselves. Rather than producing portraits of each other, Gauguin produced a *Self Portrait*. He announced by October 8 to Emile Schuffenecker that he had completed it for van Gogh, explaining that it was "quite special (complete abstraction)" and that "the colour is pretty far from nature . . . all the reds and violets streaked by flames like a furnace radiating from the eyes, seat of the struggles of the painter's thought. The whole on a pure chrome yellow background. . . ." He warned Schuffenecker that his portrait, although it looks like the notorious bandit Jean Valjean in Victor Hugo's moving realist novel *Les Misérables*, personifies "a discredited Impressionist painter." It is likely that Gauguin's reference to his own eyes, mouth and nose as appearing "like flowers in Persian carpets" was also overtly referring to his own exotic nature, as he considered himself to be half Indian. Although van Gogh admired *Les Misérables* he was struck by Gauguin's despairing image representing a prisoner, whose melancholy state was even suggested in "the flesh in the shadows" which "has gone a dismal blue." This newly adopted symbolist vision of the outward world within the group of artists at Pont-Aven can be further confirmed by the inclusion of the now believed self-portrait by Bernard in the upper right corner, the eyes of which have significantly been shut to all exterior reality.

Among them, Vincent van Gogh is the chief exponent of a multi-leveled approach to his subjects. His basic subject range is in fact limited: chiefly single figures, landscapes and still-life images. Yet each painting produced by Vincent is charged with a multiplicity of references. Apart from his known use of prototypes (for example: Japanese prints, and various Western predecessors) his work is usually oblique in its reference to a specific subject. Thus, a portrait of his close friend the postman Joseph Roulin's wife, Mme Roulin, becomes "La Berceuse" ("the Lullaby"), although the sitter had no idea that Vincent had a novel by Pierre Loti in mind when conceiving the title, or that Vincent ultimately planned to integrate this image as a central motif in a triptych in which Roulin's wife was to be flanked by equally, if symbolically obscure, life-giving sunflowers. In other words, here Realist tradition (who could wish for a more forceful likeness?), stylization according to Gauguin (especially the flower motifs on the wall), and Vincent's love of complementary colour contrasts (in this case red versus green) were amalgamated in a fusion which is the more imposing for the iconic image which it contains. The triptych as projected by Vincent in spring 1889 is thus both a product of his own imagination and the result of his long association with the idea of art as a form of religious expression.

13.
Paul Gauguin
Farmhouse with Haystack, Arles
1888
oil on canvas: 91.4 × 72.4 cm
Lent by the Indianapolis Museum of Art;
Gift in memory of William Ray Adams

Gauguin arrived in Arles from Pont-Aven on October 20, 1888 to join van Gogh for a two-month stay. Here he produced slightly over a dozen important works which displayed his newly emerged cloisonist/synthetist style. The *Farmhouse* can be singled out as an example of the artist's synthetist approach to nature, his classical restraint and intellectual approach: "Wherever I go I need a period of incubation, so that I may learn every time the essence of the plants and trees, of all nature in short, which never wishes to be understood or to yield herself." The *Farmhouse* indicates how Gauguin absorbed details from nature and how he at times combined nature with then current traditions in French modern art. In particular, his tribute to Cézanne's sense of colouration and ordered composition is noted in the farmhouse buildings and in the clearly yellow/orange, green and blue colour scheme. Gauguin's preference for ordered nature is here clearly in contradiction to van Gogh's almost pantheistic views of haystacks in Arles, which writhe in the broiling sun. It is no wonder that the two artists' violent, often "electric" discussions of their views of nature finally resulted in the Dutchman's violent self-mutilation of part of his ear and Gauguin's precipitous departure from Arles.

Such ambiguity between style and its intended content is inherent to the nature of all the artists represented in this exhibition, although they range from the extremely religious Bernard and Denis to the sceptical Gauguin and the apparently religiously unorthodox Vincent. Yet within this group not a single individual would have accorded art a less than religious function. In this respect, Vincent was a major supporter of Symbolism in painting, although he was the most surprised of all to be cited as such in Albert Aurier's inaugural article in the first issue of the *Mercure de France*.

The common philosophical denominator of Symbolist art theory was its Platonism. This is already apparent in the 1886 *Symbolist Literary Manifesto* of Jean Moréas, whose attack on the Naturalist school of literature is capped by his call for a style of art which would "clothe the idea in a perceptible form." This same anti-naturalist aesthetic provided the basis for Dujardin's definition of Cloisonism. Calling the depiction of objects as they appear in nature a chimera, Dujardin said that the aim of painting was to employ its special means, line and colour rigorously defined, to express not the appearance but rather the *sentiment* or *character* of objects. Finding this artistic ideal best represented in such "primitive" art forms as Cloisonism and Japanese prints, Dujardin hailed the embodiment of a similar mode of style in the art of Anquetin as "a symbolic conception of art." The French art critic Albert Aurier, too, was steeped in the ideational philosophy associated with the name of Plato. He first articulated his personal art theory in reference to Vincent in 1890, and the following year he identified Gauguin as an even more exemplary Symbolist artist than the then dead Vincent. Hinting that the latter's mental instability lay at the base of his artistic genius, Aurier claimed that the Dutchman was a "Hyperaesthete" who had the power to perceive "the imperceptible and secret character of lines and forms, and even more the colours, tonalities and nuances which remain invisible to healthy eyes." By the time Aurier wrote on Gauguin, his categorical definition of Symbolism in painting was associated with an art of ideas, which was produced through a general synthesis of forms and subjective perception, and which led to a decorative style in the tradition of Egyptian, Greek and late Medieval art.

A key term in this whole body of writing is *subjective deformation*. First used by Moréas, it was taken over or paraphrased by both Dujardin and Aurier. It also occurs in the writing of both Bernard and the artist Maurice Denis, who uses this phrase and its counterpart *objective deformation* as the basis of the Nabi group style with its sources, above all, in the art of Gauguin, Bernard and van Gogh. The concept that an artist is obliged to deform or distort natural appearance explains in large part not only the general stylistic reaction against Realist canons of style evident within the art of Vincent, Gauguin and their circle of friends, but also the divergencies of personal style which are equally apparent. This tolerance of multiplicity within the emerging Symbolist movement in painting is one of its most obvious characteristics, and Gauguin is known to have discouraged even his close followers Laval (pl. 22) and Jakob Meyer de Haan (pl. 16) from following his own style too closely.

Hence, in their individual artistic experiments all these artists incorporated the lessons of Cloisonism, Japanism and other "primitive" art forms but by differing means. Vincent, in particular, alternated between overt and covert references to, for example, the Japanese print. In his *Portrait of Père Tanguy* (pl. 11) and the *Japonaiserie: The Courtesan* (ill. 2) specific prints are quoted quite literally as to form, although in his choices of colour and the placement of the prints within the background composition, he effects a fundamental transformation of the original models. In contrast, whereas no one has or could find a specific source in Japanese art for *La Berceuse* (pl. 19), this did not prevent Vincent from referring to it as similar to inexpensive coloured prints, and the brush technique found in the background of *The Italian Woman* (pl. 12) is thought to have imitated the crinkled

14.
Paul Gauguin
Dramas of the Sea: Brittany
1889
zincograph on paper (black on yellow):
16.9 × 22.7 cm
Lent by the Art Institute of Chicago;
William McCallin McKee Memorial Collection

Gauguin returned to Paris in late 1888 after a disastrous two-month visit with van Gogh in Arles. He stayed briefly in the French capital with the artist Schuffenecker. Together with Bernard, Gauguin executed a series of zincographs (lithography on a zinc plate) based on experiences in Brittany and Martinique. This print has an additional literary source, Edgar Allen Poe's short story, "A Descent into the Maelstrom." The artist depicts three Breton women positioned dangerously close to a sharp precipice, their placement suggesting the precarious nature of all human existence. The artist hoped the zincographs would, in his own words, "make himself known." They were placed on sale at the famous Volpini exhibition of 1889, although it is believed none were purchased.

15.
Paul Gauguin
"Nirvana": Portrait of Meyer de Haan
1889
oil and turpentine on silk: 20 × 29 cm
Lent by the Wadsworth Atheneum, Hartford,
Connecticut; Ella Gallup Sumner and Mary
Catlin Sumner Collection

The exact date of this painting is uncertain
although the background landscape appeared as
the frontispiece to the important Volpini
exhibition catalogue in late spring, 1889. The
figure in the immediate foreground is Jakob
Meyer de Haan, a well-to-do Dutchman turned
artist. De Haan spent two years painting in
Brittany with Gauguin whom he regarded as his
master. In addition he provided Gauguin with
financial support during this difficult period.

The portrait is a highly unconventional one.
The sitter has been positioned in front of two
large (and one small) female forms. Undine, to

the right, alludes to human fertility while Eve,
with her tilted head and sensuous open mouth,
presents a metaphor of Temptation and Death.
They suggest the cycle of life and death which
brings man ultimately to a realization of the
supreme spiritual state, Nirvana. This word has
been written by the artist in the lower right
corner. The curiously slanted eyes of de Haan are
more difficult to explain. In other works by
Gauguin, these strangely treated features sym-
bolize sin and perversity – here perhaps a
reference to the sitter's liaison with his Breton
innkeeper, Marie Henry.

16.
Paul Gauguin
Christ in the Garden of Olives
c. November 1889
oil on canvas: 73 × 92 cm
Lent by the Norton Gallery and School of Art,
West Palm Beach, Florida

During 1889 Gauguin executed several large and important religious paintings. This one is unusual in its inclusion of a Gauguin self-portrait as Christ, the artist seeing his own tribulations paralleled in the Passion. Christ appears in the Garden without the comfort of his disciples. His eyes are downcast and his head bent in resignation. The "supernatural red" hair may refer to the bloody drops of sweat of the Agony while the centrally positioned tree foreshadows the Crucifixion. To the right appear Judas and his followers, about to confront the Christ-figure. Van Gogh, who rejected explicit biblical subject matter in painting, was critical of the work. "There are other means of attempting to convey an impression of anguish," he wrote his brother Théo, "without making straight for the historic garden of Gethsemane." The setting, treated in a flat and linear style reminiscent of Japanese prints, suggests the landscape of Le Pouldu on the Brittany coast. In the distance is visible the brilliant blue sea.

striations of the crepe paper on which the cheaper forms of Japanese prints were sometimes produced. Magically Vincent was able to employ these radically anti-naturalist formal innovations without completely abandoning his deep allegiance to Realist style. His portraits offer particularly good evidence of this allegiance, since all his sitters, whether *Madame Roulin*, *Père Tanguy*, *The Italian Woman* or the *Woman of Arles* (ill. 6), present us with powerfully moulded characterizations of specific human beings, who nevertheless function as emblematic of general folk types. In his landscape art, Vincent remained so fanatically loyal to the Realist-Impressionist tradition of painting out-of-doors that he several times continued painting either while the fierce Mistral winds of the region were raging, or else, at night, with candles attached to his hat to illuminate the canvas. Here too, neither his stylizations of form and outline so often reminiscent of Japanese design (see *The Langlois Bridge*, ill. 3 and *The Sower*, pl. 5) nor his intense colouration unfettered by natural appearances compromise the viewer's feeling that Vincent's sense of scale and surrounding space for the objects is just, and that he has succeeded in imbuing his chosen settings with a compelling sense of truth to nature.

Bernard's and Gauguin's allusions to earlier or exotic sources of style are usually less direct, except in a minority of instances in which a religious theme is treated overtly. Employment of such imagery was at first quite hesitant, and Gauguin's famous 1888 *Vision after the Sermon* (pl. 7), for all its Japanese elements of style and Cloisonist colouration (Gauguin wished to donate this work to a church, thus hinting at an analogy with stained glass windows), remains a depiction of Breton folk life insofar as the scene pretends to represent a collective vision of church goers after hearing a sermon concerning Jacob's struggle with the angel. Even in the *Yellow Christ* (pl. 24) and *Calvary* (pl. 23) Gauguin insists upon extant local religious monuments from the neighborhood of Pont-Aven and places them within identifiable nearby settings, although he intentionally confuses matters by not depicting the monuments in their actual locations. The result is a quasi-iconic form of painting which so mingles medievalizing religious imagery with contemporary life in rural Brittany that it is impossible to decide whether sacred or profane art is intended. In such paintings as *Christ in the Garden of Olives* (ill. 16) where his own features appear as the forsaken Christ, and *The Loss of Virginity* (ill. 17) where the supine figure of a young girl represents his mistress yet also recalls traditional tomb sculpture, Gauguin's sources attain another level of complexity and self-identification. In his own view of life and art, the two were so intermingled that for Gauguin, distinction of past and present, sacred and profane, and realistic versus stylized artistic depiction, by the late 1880s assumed diminished importance.

17.
Paul Gauguin
The Loss of Virginity: La Perte de Pucelage
c. winter 1890-91
oil on canvas: 90 × 130 cm
Lent by the Chrysler Museum at Norfolk, Virginia; Gift of Walter P. Chrysler Jr.

Little is known about the origins of this large and significant painting. Probably worked on in Paris in early 1891, its Breton landscape suggests execution at least in part from memory, a technique strongly advocated by Gauguin. The reclining female nude, reminiscent of both funerary sculpture and the dead Christ, represents Virginity, indicated by the small flower in her right hand. Emotionless, the young girl embraces a fox, a symbol of perversity – perhaps Gauguin himself. In fact, the artist's mistress, the "innocent" Juliette Huet, posed for the figure. Following Gauguin's departure for Tahiti, she bore him a child. The work is characteristic of the painter's Synthetist style: emotions and ideas have been presented through a cloisonist simplification of outline and the use of flat areas of saturated colour.

18.
Emile Bernard (1868-1941)
Self Portrait dedicated to Vincent
end of September 1888
oil on canvas: 46 × 55 cm
Lent by the Rijksmuseum Vincent van Gogh,
Amsterdam

Both Gauguin's *Self Portrait "Les Misérables"*
(ill. 12) and Bernard's *Self Portrait* arrived in
one package in Arles by October 7 and Vincent
immediately expressed to Bernard how these two
images had warmed his heart greatly "to see the
two faces again." In precisely such a self portrait
by Bernard, van Gogh believed, lay the future
and the means by which they must win the
public over. In contrast to the tormented but
confident *"Les Misérables,"* Vincent was
especially impressed by the young Bernard's
sensitive head which captured so remarkably the
"inner vision of a painter" in a "few abrupt
tones, a few dark lines." Surely Bernard's timid
image set off in pale delicate tones recalled the
artist's own personal sense of intimidation and
inadequacy towards the strongly assertive and
artistically mature Gauguin – a thought which he
had confided to Vincent by late September. Van
Gogh's reference to Bernard's portrait having the
distinction of a "real, real Manet" not only
referred to Bernard's use of the earlier artist's
inherent linear simplification and aesthetically
considered compositions, but confirmed the note
of total modernity which Bernard interjected by
his strikingly modern grey felt hat which
contrasts sharply with Gauguin's bohemian
beret. That Bernard may have had Manet's
Portrait of Emile Zola in mind may account for
this radically urbane image of the young artist in
his studio at Pont-Aven. The centrally placed
abstract image of Gauguin has been argued to
represent a self portrait by the artist, and is
substantiated by Bernard's personal hesitation
"to do Gauguin." As in Bernard's self image in
"Les Misérables" here again Gauguin's eyes,
which according to symbolist thought expressed
the seat of the thoughts, have been firmly shut to
outward nature in order to glean sustenance from
his own "inner visions."

This tendency to intermingle artistic sources and modes of representation was also characteristic of Gauguin's friend, Bernard. This young artist was equally impressed by Japanese and Western Medieval art, which were freely mixed and submerged in a personal style that by summer 1888 may well, as he later maintained, have induced Gauguin to a more rigorous examination of what amounted to Cloisonist principles. Thus Bernard's *Breton Women in the Meadow* (pl. 9) with its groups of figures placed against a flat green background is not only in itself an archetype of Cloisonist style, but the presumed basis for the Medievalizing aspect of Gauguin's *Vision after the Sermon*. Bernard's example admittedly contains no direct reference to an event in sacred history, but his later reference to it as representing a "Pardon" or annual pilgrimage festival at Pont-Aven is supported by the presence of two little priests, upper left, and the prominence of the costumes and headdress of the Breton women. In a letter of 1889 from Gauguin in Brittany to Vincent, Gauguin diagrammed and explained what he considered the religious symbolism (namely, a cross) inherent to the headdress of the Breton peasantry. There is little reason to doubt that Bernard shared in this identification as well. Indeed, Bernard had depicted his own sister, the pious Madeleine, reclining like a tomb effigy in the "Bois d'Amour" of Pont-Aven, similar in position to that of the girl in *Loss of Virginity* (ill. 17), which inescapably implies some indebtedness by Gauguin to Bernard's precedent. In any case, by 1889 both men were consciously employing medievalizing imagery in their art, albeit scarcely in a manner which was comprehensible to normal church patronage. Whereas Vincent outspokenly deplored this new turn in the art of his two friends, the previous year he himself had produced a large watercolour copy (pl. 10) as tribute to Bernard's *Breton Women* which Gauguin had brought with him from Pont-Aven to Arles.

19.
Emile Bernard
Portrait of the Artist's Grandmother
fall 1887
oil on canvas: 53 × 64 cm
Lent by the Rijksmuseum Vincent van Gogh,
Amsterdam

The sitter is Bernard's maternal grandmother,
the widowed Madame Sophie Bodin, who
operated a laundry establishment in Lille and
who by late August-September 1887 had joined
the artist's family in their new living quarters in
Asnières. Bernard's deep attachment and admiration for his grandmother was estalished early in
his life when for financial reasons he was left in
her care in Lille. Several canvases and sketches
exist of her mature features as tribute by Bernard
to the backing she offered him during years of
bitter parental opposition to the artist's chosen

profession. Van Gogh described this portrait to
his sister Wilhelmina as follows, "It is the portrait
of his grandmother, very old, blind in one eye;
the background is the wall of a room covered
with chocolate-coloured wallpaper and a completely white bed." The strong broad areas of
colour and simplified outlines document Bernard's radically achieved sense of abstraction
within the group of the "Petit Boulevard" by late
1887. Van Gogh in Paris had exchanged a
self-portrait for this canvas and later in Arles he
questioned Bernard when he would show
"studies of such vigorous soundness again."
Although Vincent saw this portrait in terms of
Daumier's virile realism, Bernard's own sources
for the portrait possibly embraced also Japanese
prints with their depiction of the similarly austere
features of actors.

20.
Emile Bernard
Lane in Brittany
July 1888
watercolour inscribed "Esquisse" and
"Pont-Aven:" 30.5 × 20 cm
Lent by the Rijksmuseum Vincent van Gogh,
Amsterdam

At the end of July 1888 van Gogh received "ten
drawings" from Bernard who was then working
in St. Briac in Brittany. The Dutch artist was very
pleased with this watercolour in particular, which
he described as an "avenue of plane trees on the
seashore with two women chatting in the
foreground and people strolling about." The
inscription "Pont-Aven" on the drawing has
been argued to suggest that Bernard had possibly
visited Pont-Aven before joining Gauguin there
by mid August. On the other hand, Bernard

could have been working from memory of his earlier trip to Pont-Aven in 1886. In any case, *Lane in Brittany* substantiates Bernard's insistent claim to have produced a highly decorative and simplified cloisonist style by late July 1888, before his significant contact with Gauguin in August. Heavy dark contour lines act almost as lead enclosures around bright greens and blues, producing a striking stained glass effect. Bernard here and Gauguin later were deeply moved by the expressive potentials inherent in the mysterious Breton costumes, especially the medievalizing large white bonnets and starched white collars. A striking comparison is to be noted between this cloisonist watercolour and Bernard's famous *Breton Women in the Meadow* (pl. 9) produced a month or two later.

21.
Emile Bernard
Christ at the foot of the Cross: Lamentation
1890
oil on canvas: 90 × 150 cm
Lent by Clément Altarriba, Paris

Bernard's devout catholicism is documented by the artist as having occurred during his first voyage on foot through Brittany, where Gothic cathedrals with their stained glass and sculpture likely made him a "saint from Brittany" ready to fight for the Catholic church. Such nostalgic catholic yearning for the Middle Ages became increasingly manifested in Bernard's *oeuvre*, creating a turning point from his earlier fresh cloisonist subjects. By late 1889, van Gogh received in St. Rémy a series of photographs of such recent canvases as *The Adoration of the Magi*, *Christ in the Garden of Olives* and *The*

Annunciation. These biblical subjects with their mannered abstractions were mourned by van Gogh as being counterfeit and affected. He urged Bernard to look to nature and to abandon abstraction which is "enchanted ground . . . and one soon finds oneself up against a stone wall." The *Lamentation* of the following year shows that Vincent's pleas went unheeded; Bernard completely abandoned naturalism for such symbolic and Gothic representations of melancholic suffering of the Middle Ages.

SOTHEBY & CO.

Vincent's opposition to the use of religious or other "literary"symbolism in contemporary painting points up a divergence within our group of artists about the use to which shared stylistic innovations were to be put. Whereas van Gogh's own rejection of overt symbolism never compromised his wish to imbue his paintings with deeply felt spiritual values, Anquetin's and Lautrec's art was increasingly devoted to depictions of urban – and urbane – secular activities centred in the everyday or nightlife world of Paris. To Bernard's consternation both men, who enjoyed private means of support, themselves entered into, as well as depicted in art, that world of high fashion bohemia which is remembered today as characteristic of Paris in the gay nineties. Anquetin's renderings of elegantly dressed women and smartly groomed horses hurrying across a bridge over the Seine (pl. 29) or along the Champs Elysée (ill. 23), and the depictions which both he and Lautrec produced of the circus, café, cabaret or concert hall interiors of the Montmartre amusement district, may be considered the principal harbingers of the international Art Nouveau movement both for their mannered distortion of figural style and because of the iconography of gay yet fragile amusement among the *demi-monde* which they epitomize. Lautrec's purest use of Cloisonist style in fact occurred in his lithographic posters of the 1890s, one of which contains an image of the famous dancer-singer Jane Avril which was used in Anquetin's final major painting in this genre, the *Dance Hall at the Moulin Rouge* (pl. 32).

22.
Louis Anquetin (1861-1932)
The Kiosk: Boulevard de Clichy
1886
oil on canvas: 44.2 × 36.5 cm
Lent by Mr. and Mrs. Arthur G. Altschul, New York

The early work of Louis Anquetin remains little known. Very few of his works which were listed in exhibition catalogues of the 1880s have been published, and many canvases from his formative years are thought to have been destroyed by the artist or lost. A rare example of Anquetin's researches into Impressionism is to be seen in *The Kiosk*. This hitherto unknown work was presented to Bernard by the artist. In fact it is from Bernard's testimony that we learn how Anquetin's colouristic researches led him to visit Claude Monet in the summer of 1886, a visit which helped lighten Anquetin's palette considerably. From the same account by Bernard we can now identify the subject with certainty as having been painted from the first floor of a popular café on the Boulevard de Clichy which was assiduously frequented by pupils of Cormon's atelier. Despite Anquetin's evident debts to Impressionism, we can see in this canvas the commencement of a strong sense of design and linearity which anticipates his cloisonist style of 1887.

23.
Louis Anquetin
The Rond Point of the Champs Elysée
1889
pastel on paper: 153 × 99 cm
Lent by a private collection, Paris

Anquetin was very early characterized by his peers and critics as an extremely versatile and promising artist whose predominant artistic temperament was that of a constant inventor of new styles. By 1888, the critic Edouard Dujardin had baptised the young artist's innovatively simplified style as "Cloisonisme" because of the strong outlines surrounding each vibrant flat tone in his paintings, reminiscent of stained glass effects. *The Rond Point* remains an example of the artist's continued interest in the cloisonist style in 1889. By this time, however, after Anquetin's move from the "Petit Boulevard" area, his close artistic ties with Bernard were waning. This move produced a radical shift from his earlier simpler subject matter. Elegant Parisian scenes with boldly stylized horses as found in *The Rond Point* became a recurrent theme.

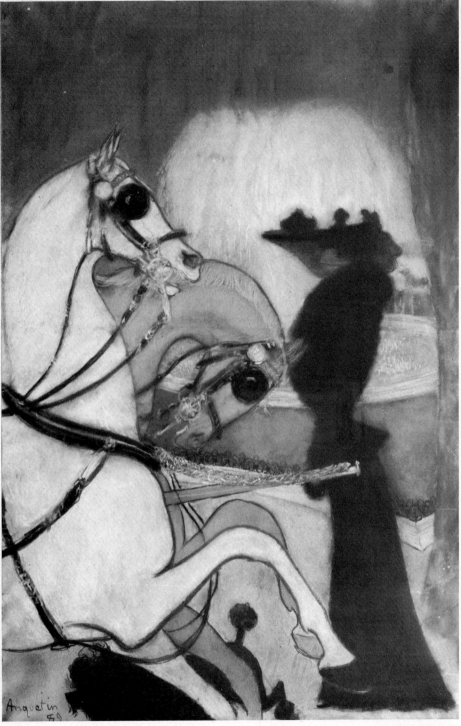

24.
Louis Anquetin
Female Head in Profile with Blue Hat: "La Goulue"
1890
pastel: 37.5 × 40.5 cm
Lent by a private collection, Paris

The identity of the subject of this pastel, *La Goulue* (The Glutton), remains uncertain. Anquetin was noted for his sharp eye for character and frequented bohemian night life in Montmartre and Parisian out-door sites in order to search out new models. This striking pastel represents Anquetin's talent to mix satire with sophisticated elegance. It becomes evident that by 1890 the artist still retained a bold decorative quality in his portraits of fashionable Paris life.

25.
Henri de Toulouse-Lautrec (1864-1901)
Rice Powder: Poudre de Riz
1887
oil on canvas: 65 × 58 cm
Lent by the Rijksmuseum Vincent van Gogh,
Amsterdam

From Arles van Gogh anxiously inquired of his
brother Théo whether "Lautrec had finished his
picture of a woman leaning on a little table in a
café," which he had seen unfinished at the time
of his departure from Paris. In fact Théo had
purchased this canvas from Lautrec by January,
but evidently allowed Lautrec to send it to his
debut exhibit with *Les Vingt* in Brussels. Like
van Gogh's earlier canvas of *Agostina Segatori*
(ill. 1) which Lautrec would have known,
Lautrec presents a similarly posed image of
urbane modernity within the café society of
Montmartre. Significantly, Vincent understood
this subject's artificiality and wished to further
contrast the powdered elegance of Lautrec's
model by juxtaposing it next to *Patience Escalier*,
his own rugged sunburned peasant portrait of a
shepherd from the Camargue hills near Arles.

26.
Henri de Toulouse-Lautrec
The Laundress
1888
brush and ink heightened with lead on scratch
board: 76.2 × 62.9 cm
Lent by The Cleveland Museum of Art;
Gift of Hanna Fund

By 1888 Lautrec's work began to evolve towards
a highly expressive yet simplified style. His
contacts with the artists of the "Petit Boulevard,"
namely van Gogh, Bernard and Anquetin,
enabled him to develop a personal form of
cloisonism. Through study of Japanese prints and
artists such as Degas, Lautrec firmly established a
break from his earlier Impressionist style. *The
Laundress* is one of four drawings which Lautrec
designed to illustrate an article by Emile Michelet
on "L'Été à Paris" which appeared in the
journal *Paris Illustré* on July 7, 1888. This large
brush and ink drawing exemplifies Lautrec's
meticulous attention for detail as well as his
ability to grasp the essential character of the
figure and the surrounding objects. Lautrec was
an avid rider and, like his close friend Anquetin,
frequently introduces the horse motif within his
Parisian scenes. Significantly the artist has chosen
to depict a boulevard scene of Montmartre in a
raking-angle perspective not unlike that of
Anquetin's *Avenue de Clichy* (pl. 2).

27.
Charles Laval (1862-1894)
Self Portrait dedicated to Vincent
1888
oil on canvas: 50 × 60 cm
Lent by the Rijksmuseum Vincent van Gogh,
Amsterdam

On December 2, 1888 van Gogh wrote Théo:
"You will be pleased to hear that we have an
addition to the collection of portraits of artists. A
self portrait by Laval, extremely good." Almost a
year later Vincent seemed not to have forgotten
this striking portrait of Gauguin's inseparable
companion and specifically recalled to Théo
Laval's "frank look." Very little remains known
of this mysterious artist's life and work; by 1894
his tubercular condition induced an early death.
Some time in 1886 Laval had encountered
Gauguin in Pont-Aven and from then on
continued to be highly influenced by the latter's
art. Gauguin had painted an earlier portrait of his
friend in 1886 (also in the exhibition) before both
men departed for Panama and Martinique. By
summer 1888, Laval had joined Gauguin in
Pont-Aven whence he produced this *Self
Portrait* for Vincent. Laval's image was evidently
conceived as an accompaniment to both
Gauguin's and Bernard's portrait exchanges with
van Gogh. At the same time the starkness of this
Self Portrait against so obviously a full-blown
landscape background can be considered a
precedent for several portraits which both
Gauguin and Vincent executed in Arles later in
the year.

The second direction in which the Cloisonist experimentation of the late 1880s developed was that epitomized by the Nabi movement, in which an overt revival of religious art was a major ideal. This is best seen in the work of the founding Nabi spirits Paul Sérusier and Maurice Denis. These painters were originally inspired by both the style and the occasional Medievalizing iconography of Gauguin to evolve a group movement whose stylistic orientation was as congenial to, as its implied return to Catholicism was inimicable to, Gauguin's own temperament. One should not hereby suppose that even such religiously devout painters as Denis and Sérusier were dedicated to a return to an orthodox Christian art pure and simple. Sérusier's famous *The Bois d'Amour at Pont-Aven* (ill. 28), subtitled *The Talisman*, which he executed in late summer 1888 under direct supervision by Gauguin, had only the most general of romantic religious associations, and, if so, these more with Bernard's sepulchral image of *Madeleine in the Bois d'Amour* than with any painting then executed by Gauguin. It was the latter's landscape style which had the greatest impact upon the career of Sérusier, whose own mature style was informed as much by his varied interests in Platonic philosophy, the Theosophic spiritualist movement and a learned study of Breton religious folklore as by an interest in reviving earlier Christian forms of art.

Denis was undoubtedly the most devoted Christian and Catholic among the Nabi membership, yet his own mixture of the sacred and profane, of the past and present in his iconography remains perhaps closer to the spirit of Gauguin's *Yellow Christ* than would prove characteristic of the Nabi group as a whole. His little *The Way to Calvary* (ill. 30), for example, combines a brush technique reminiscent of Sérusier's *Talisman* with an anacronistic use of nun's garb for the female figures and an ambiguity in the scene depicted (Veronica only wiped Christ's face with her cloth, scarcely embraced him). It is clearly less Medievalizing in style or iconography than Bernard's *Lamentation* (ill. 21) with its Gothicizing figural stylizations and more or less orthodox iconography. Finally, Gauguin's indirect or ambiguous references to Christian iconographic tradition were so powerful a stimulus within his circle of friends that even Meyer de Haan, a Jewish artist, could paint his presumed mistress Marie Henry and her child (*Motherhood*, ill. 29) in a manner inevitably recalling the Christian Madonna and Child. All in all, the intentionally veiled meaning of Gauguin's "religious" paintings produced a heterogeneous collection of offspring even within his own immediate family of followers, and the influence of these paintings was to extend into the far reaches of the international Art Nouveau.

S.P.A.D.E.M.

refers to the fact that he painted it directly under supervision by Gauguin, who agreed to give this leading student at the Academie Julian in Paris a quite obviously anti-academic lesson in painting. According to Denis' account, Gauguin advised him to abjure the use of mixed or tonal colours for pure colours from the merchant's tube. This idea in turn relates to Denis' own published art theory of 1890: "Remember that a painting, before it is a battle horse, a nude woman or some anecdote, is in essence a flat surface covered over with colours in a certain order." Given the close association between Sérusier and Denis in founding the Nabi association, there could be no greater single token of their acknowledged indebtedness to the model of Gauguin than this tiny magical painting.

29.
Jakob Meyer de Haan (1852-1895)
Motherhood: Marie Henry and her Child
fall 1889
oil on canvas: 73 × 60 cm
Lent by a private collection, Switzerland

The subject of this painting is the purported mistress of Meyer de Haan, and she kept the inn at the Breton coastal hamlet of Le Pouldu where he and Gauguin lodged for much of 1889-90. It is known that the Dutch artist painted this portrait of Marie and her first daughter Lea without showing it to Gauguin until finished. Gauguin was so pleased with the progress it evinced in de Haan's art – doubtless in adapting to his own precepts of style – that Gauguin made and himself decorated a frame for it (unfortunately now lost). It was then hung in the most prominent place in the common dining hall of the inn, which he and de Haan were in the process of decorating with their own works of art.

The popular title "Maternity," although not founded on any early reference by either artist or Marie Henry, does suggest the quasi-religious connotations of Madonna and Child with which de Haan, an apparently learned and free-thinking Jew, wished to invest this depiction of a woman he doubtless felt affection for, perhaps already loved. The background farmyard setting with hay could not have been seen from a window of the inn, and therefore is most likely both a reference to the subject and style of a type of painting being produced by Gauguin at the time and a further enrichment of the general theme of the earth's and this mother's fecundity.

28.
Paul Sérusier (1864-1927)
The Talisman: The Bois d'Amour at Pont-Aven
September-October 1888
oil on wood: 27 × 22 cm
Lent by the family of Maurice Denis, Alençon, France

An inscription in French on the back of this painting reads "Made under the direction of Gauguin. P. Sérusier, 1888," and we know from an account by the artist's friend Denis, who received this famous little painting as a gift, that the artist himself called it "The Talisman." The alternative title is more descriptive, giving the picturesque riverside setting at Pont-Aven, which was called *Bois d'Amour* ("Woods of Love") since couples seen strolling there would be presumed to be courting. Both titles suggest the mystical and magic powers which would be attributed to works of art by Sérusier, Denis and their associates in the Nabi movement. The artist's inscription on the back more specifically

30.
Maurice Denis (1870-1943)
The Way to Calvary
November 1889
oil on canvas: 41 × 32.5 cm
Lent by a private collection

The extreme simplification of contour outlines and flattening of both figures and landscape background make this one of the most Cloisonist style paintings in Denis' career, although its muted colouration, probably chosen to conform with the dolorous theme depicted, is less in keeping with the bright hues of medieval tradition. The inscribed November 1889 date is the earliest recorded on any known example of this style in the painter's *oeuvre*. It places the painting at that moment in his career when he had just received from Sérusier, who had been working at Le Pouldu with Gauguin, the former's first recorded statement of an art theory which claimed to be based on the "immutable principles" found in Japanese, Gothic and Egyptian art and which called for stress on the "harmony of line and colour." Not that these principles came unannounced to Denis, who had previously held long discussions on art with his friend Sérusier, whose *Talisman* (ill. 28) he already knew, if not already owned.

The style of this particular painting, despite an indebtedness to the Pont-Aven school of Gauguin and Bernard which he was the first to admit, nonetheless has a quality of quiet elegance peculiar to Denis himself. While representing one of the most proto-abstract canvases in French painting of the late 1880s, it also suggests the love of the thirteenth to fifteenth century Italian primitives which would be more fully manifested in his subsequent production.

How was this group activity situated within and affected the Post-Impressionist period in France and elsewhere? An initial supposition is that the so-called Pont-Aven or Synthetist school of painting was formed only immediately upon the meeting between Bernard and Gauguin in the summer of 1888 in Pont-Aven, with the chief purpose of forming a common stylistic front against the Neo-Impressionist opposition. Attractive in its simplicity though the supposition may be, it obscures the complexity of historical origins and shared attitudes with the Pointillists which actually existed. As numerous paintings in the current exhibition reveal, all of these supposedly anti-Pointillist artists actually passed through a Neo-Impressionist phase before achieving a mature personal style or else a form of structured Impressionism analogous to it. Both Vincent and Anquetin employed Pointillism and its related colour laws to create styles similarly antagonistic to any residue of Impressionist luminosity, even if Vincent's personal use of Cloisonist emphasis on a distinction between contour outlines and areas of saturated colour left room for a frequent use of complementary colour contrasts. These were virtually ruled out by Gauguin and Bernard. They nonetheless had either experimented in Pointillist technique or appropriated principles of structured compositions from the Neo-Impressionists, before proceeding to their own form of Cloisonist-Synthetist style. Apart from the vexed questions of who first achieved a fully mature Cloisonist style, and of borrowings back and forth in its mutual creation, to single out one painting, or only very few, as "the breakthrough" or "purest" example(s) is less important than to appreciate the special character of an individual's achievement or approach. Not only Bernard's *Breton Women* and Gauguin's *Vision*, but also Anquetin's *Mower* and *Avenue de Clichy*, Lautrec's *At the Circus Fernando* (pl. 30) and several paintings by Vincent from as early as his Paris years might reasonably be put forward for the laurel wreath of first or best example of the Cloisonist style.

The same point may be made regarding the uses which individual artists, whether those here exhibited or not, make of their sources of inspiration. All of the artists discussed became interested in Japanese art, many in one or another form of Medieval art, and some in such art traditions further afield as those of ancient Egypt or other "primitive" societies. This relative de-emphasis on the Renaissance to Neo-classic periods in itself reveals a widespread attitude in late nineteenth century *avant-garde* French painting. Certainly Gauguin's well-known attachment to Ingres and Vincent's to Delacroix should remind us that the deep-seated controversy between proponents of classical standards (where line prevailed) and of expressive colour was alive and healthy within even their own temporal and physical artistic ambience. This consideration does not diminish the fact that both Gauguin and Vincent and their closest colleagues were more interested in realigning Western artistic tradition toward a wider range of stylistic alternatives than was imminent within this tradition in the immediate past. Their very eclecticism in the use of sources was itself a sign of the times, a phenomenon which would become the standard rather than the exception by the turn of the century. The quality with which eclecticism is employed, rather than the fact thereof, provides a better standard of judgment than any compilation for or against such a usage.

The art of Japan, to take the most obvious instance, was least of all something imposed from without, considering the reluctance with which that country encouraged cultural ties with the West. Instead, modern French art employed the Japanese artistic heritage with great fecundity precisely because of the variety of applications to which it was prone. Ceramic design, the graphic arts and painting were equally susceptible to its influence. Neither van Gogh, Gauguin, Bernard, Anquetin, nor Lautrec had the "right answer" for incorporating the styles of the East and the West. One might say that they all had the right answer, although not in equal proportion according to the specific applications which were attempted. Ultimately its effect in liberating European art from the straitjacket of one major movement succeeding another without recourse to alternative traditions equals the contribution this seemingly unfathomable well of inspiration provided to individual artists. Within the "Impressionists of the Little Boulevard" this one influence was the most widespread, but it did not prevent a range of adaptations which would have seemed unthinkable even among the Impressionists, who beginning with Manet had done most to employ Japanese sources in the service of Western "high art." These applications ranged from Vincent's so-called copies of specific Japanese prints to his almost clinical study of a moth (ill. 7) which he saw as a mixture somehow of both Oriental and scientific observation. This one question of just when, how and why such a contribution from a specific (in fact, in its homeland, modestly appreciated) source occurred underscores the intricacy with which both professionals and laymen in the field of art must approach the viewing of the works of art here exhibited.

The multiplicity and ambiguity of artistic usages manifest in this exhibition offer both a challenge and an opportunity to the viewer. It is not only the scholar who will, not to say must, be interested in this present selection and juxtaposition of works of art. The average visitor must also be expected to look for similiarities and differences, if he or she is to achieve a maximum enrichment of aesthetic response to and knowledge about this rich area of artistic creativity. Because of the number of artists selected and the variety of personal style and subject matter which has been included, the method of display inevitably represents one choice among many. The viewer is therefore encouraged to seek his or her own pleasure and enlightenment by personally selected comparisons, rather than following the normal sequence of works of art from one wall to the next. With the chronological span and the number of artists represented so consciously restricted, this approach is particularly rewarding precisely because one is assured that the relationships discovered result from a combination of intensely personal and historically significant factors.

This exhibition may best be described as an intentionally conservative yet decidedly unconventional enterprise. It is conservative insofar as its appeal rests upon such established luminaries as Vincent van Gogh, Paul Gauguin and Henri de Toulouse-Lautrec. It is adventurous insofar as a significant body of the art presented was executed by such lesser-known artists as Emile Bernard, Louis Anquetin, Charles Laval, Jakob Meyer de Haan, Paul Sérusier and Maurice Denis, although several of these can only be termed lesser-known by dint of comparison with such luminaries as van Gogh and Gauguin. It is to be hoped that among other things this exhibition modifies the idea of major or minor artists, since it may well be that each artist occasionally and more likely often strays into the pastures of the other. One is therefore best advised to use the present experience as a get-acquainted period with the familiar and less than familiar, with the expectation that further acquaintance will produce more intimate results. As the works of art presented here fade from memory, it is certain that the spectator's visit to other museums and art galleries will have been enriched by a careful and inventive viewing of the current exhibition. The plastic arts are, after all, defined between imaginative creator and viewers.

We have purposefully chosen a narrow focus on one of the most prolific of Western art movements. In contrast to the "one-man retrospective," an infinitely less complicated matter to consider, we were determined to present a variety of artists and works of art which, though often discussed yet rarely seen together, were clearly conceived within the same cultural crucible. Van Gogh, Gauguin, Lautrec *et al.* are among the most significant influences on the origins and development of twentieth century painting. They are not so susceptible to interpretation as harbingers of things to come, as they are outstanding and artistically supreme representatives of their time. Whatever intimations of Matisse or Picasso one might wish here to discover, the interrelationships among these artists in Paris of the late 1880s remain its essential focus.

Chronology

1886

JANUARY-FEBRUARY
Emile Bernard, Louis Antequin and Toulouse-Lautrec work at the atelier Cormon on the Boulevard de Clichy in Montmartre. The three artists explore modern art in French galleries, visit the Louvre and frequent the paint shop of Julien "Père" Tanguy.

MARCH
Vincent van Gogh joins his art dealer brother Théo in Paris. Bernard quarrels with Fernand Cormon over his progressive colour tendencies and quits the atelier for good.

APRIL
Paul Gauguin experiences great financial hardships and works as a bill poster in Paris.
Bernard departs on his walking tour for Brittany. In the spring or fall van Gogh works at the atelier Cormon.

MAY-JUNE
The eighth and last Impressionist Exhibition is held in Paris. Paul Gauguin exhibits 19 canvases and Georges Seurat shows his major pointillist canvas *Afternoon on the Island of the Grande-Jatte*.
Van Gogh paints still lifes of flowers and the surrounding Montmartre district with an increasingly lightened palette. Vincent and Théo move in June to a larger apartment on 54 rue Lepic in Montmartre.

SUMMER
Anquetin leaves Cormon's atelier after a student uprising and briefly visits Claude Monet at Giverny before spending the summer in his native village of Etrépagny in Normandy.
Paul Gauguin in June visits Pont-Aven for the first time and stays at the Inn of Marie Jeanne Gloanec. Here he befriends the artist Charles Laval. Gauguin paints still basically Impressionist canvases.
In July Bernard is working in St. Briac. The end of July at Concarneau he meets the artist Schuffenecker who gives him a card of introduction to Paul Gauguin. Bernard arrives in Pont-Aven in August for a two-month stay and makes his first acquaintance with Gauguin and Laval. Bernard works in a quasi-pointillist style.

FALL
(August-September) Seurat and Paul Signac exhibit pointillist canvases at the Salon des Artistes Indépendants in Paris. Seurat's canvas *Afternoon on the Island of the Grande-Jatte* is shown once again.
Late September Bernard returns to Paris and sees van Gogh working at Cormon's. Soon thereafter Bernard makes the Dutch artist's acquaintance at the shop of Père Tanguy.
In September Lautrec sees his first drawings published in *Le Courrier Français* and exhibits for the first time (October-December).

WINTER
In November Gauguin has arrived in Paris and works on his first ceramics.
A close relationship develops between van Gogh and Bernard. The latter artist and Lautrec attend social gatherings at Louis Antequin's lodgings on 84 avenue de Clichy in Montmartre.
Anquetin works on a major canvas representing the interior of the cabaret *Le Mirliton* in Montmartre owned by the writer and singer Aristide Bruant. Both Antequin and Lautrec regularly frequent this bohemian night spot where several of Lautrec's canvases are permanently displayed by the owner.

1887

FEBRUARY-APRIL
Close contacts between Anquetin, Lautrec and Bernard. Anquetin and Bernard experiment with pointillist colour theories and style.
Bernard exhibits some pointillist works. Both Bernard and Anquetin visit the studio of the Neo-Impressionist artist Paul Signac.
Van Gogh organizes an exhibition of Japanese prints at the café *Le Tambourin* which influences Bernard and Anquetin enormously.
Lautrec does a pastel portrait of van Gogh. Paul Gauguin and Charles Laval depart for Panama and Martinique on April 9th.
At the end of April Bernard is working in Normandy.

MAY-JUNE
Van Gogh in Paris works with a quasi-pointillist style, painting at times in the outskirts of Asnières with Paul Signac, who leaves Paris by the end of May.
Bernard is in St. Briac for two months producing highly simplified canvases. Here he meets the symbolist art critic Albert Aurier.

SUMMER
Anquetin is working in his native village of Etrépagny. He produces his first significant cloisonist canvas *The Mower* (pl. 4).
Lautrec spends his summer in Arcachon on the Atlantic coast in the south of France.

FALL

Bernard returns to Paris by September and Anquetin arrives as well. These two artists and van Gogh experience close artistic contacts.

Bernard and Anquetin continue to paint mature cloisonist canvases.

Van Gogh paints two portraits of Père Tanguy. Sometime during October-November the first and only exhibition of the "Petit Boulevard" artists is held under the stimulus of van Gogh at a popular restaurant on the Avenue de Clichy in Montmartre. This exhibition, which includes canvases by van Gogh, Bernard, Anquetin and Lautrec, is visited by several avant-garde artists including Georges Seurat.

In November Gauguin returns alone from Martinique. He visits this exhibition and meets van Gogh.

WINTER

Gauguin lodges with the Schuffenecker family and begins his association with the Gallery Boussod and Valadon operated by Théo van Gogh.

In December, Gauguin exhibits there three paintings and five ceramics.

Bernard, van Gogh, Théo, Gauguin, Camille and Lucien Pissarro discuss the possibility of a Society of Impressionists.

1888

JANUARY-FEBRUARY

Gauguin in Paris produces no new paintings and works on his ceramics.

Van Gogh experiences during the winter both great physical problems aggravated by alcohol, and psychological tension with his brother Théo.

In January Anquetin exhibits three cloisonist works in the offices of Edouard Dujardin's journal *La Revue Indépendante*. February 9th Gauguin departs for Pont-Aven.

In February Anquetin exhibits eight works at the exhibition of *Les Vingt* in Brussels including his *Mower* (pl. 4) and *Avenue de Clichy* (pl. 2).

Lautrec shows in the same exhibition twelve works including *At the Circus Fernando* (pl. 30).

February 20, van Gogh has arrived in Arles and begins to experience the sensation of having found Japan in the south of France.

MARCH

Anquetin exhibits the above-mentioned eight works at the Salon des Artistes Indépendants in Paris.

Van Gogh shows three works at the same exhibition.

Edouard Dujardin reviews Anquetin's paintings in this exhibition and baptises the latter's new style "cloisonism" in his pioneering article "Le Cloisonisme" in *La Revue Indépendante* (March 1st).

Gauguin, plagued by sickness, corresponds with Vincent and Théo van Gogh.

MAY

Bernard arrives in St. Briac where he works for three months and corresponds with Vincent, sending the latter several important highly cloisonist watercolours including the *Lane in Brittany* (ill. 20).

SUMMER

Early June, Vincent and Théo propose that Gauguin stay with Vincent in his newly rented "Yellow House" (pl. 14).

In July Lautrec has four drawings published in *Paris Illustré* including *The Laundress* (ill. 26).

Early July Gauguin agrees to go to Arles to stay with van Gogh.

Charles Laval joins Gauguin in Pont-Aven.

Anquetin, suffering severe bouts of rheumatism, works sporadically in Etrépagny.

Around August 7-14 Bernard arrives in Pont-Aven, bringing with him his recent cloisonist works from St. Briac.

Bernard's sister Madeleine joins her brother in Pont-Aven and becomes the adored Muse for both Bernard and Gauguin.

Gauguin and Bernard paint portraits of her and both Gauguin and Laval become infatuated by her fresh innocence.

SEPTEMBER

A month of intense creativity begins for Bernard. He executes his famous canvas *Breton Women in the Meadow* (pl. 9). Gauguin then produces *The Vision after the Sermon* (pl. 7).

In late September Bernard paints his *Self Portrait: dedicated to Vincent* (ill. 18) and Gauguin executes his *Self Portrait: Les Misérables* (ill. 12) for van Gogh.

Van Gogh paints his *Yellow House* (pl. 14).

OCTOBER-NOVEMBER

Early October Vincent receives, in Arles, Bernard's and Gauguin's self-portraits.

Van Gogh paints his *Bedroom* (pl. 15).

Around early October Paul Sérusier meets Gauguin in Pont-Aven and there paints *The Talisman* (ill. 28).

Sometime this year Sérusier meets for the first time his life-long friend Maurice Denis at the Academie Julian in Paris and thereafter helps found the Nabi group movement. Meyer de Haan arrives from the Netherlands and is befriended by Théo van Gogh.

On October 23rd Gauguin joins van Gogh in Arles. Both artists begin to work together, often exchanging opposing ideas on painting after the imagination rather than from nature directly.

In November, Bernard is back in Paris.

Gauguin produces mature Synthetist works, e.g. *Misères Humaines* (pl. 25) and *Women at Arles: The Mistral* (pl. 26).

DECEMBER

By mid-December, Gauguin considers himself temperamentally incompatible as a companion to Vincent.

On or about December 23rd occurs the confrontation which led to Vincent's self-mutilation of part of the ear.

Théo arrives in Arles to find van Gogh in the hospital and stays over Christmas.

Gauguin goes back with Théo to Paris.

1889

JANUARY

On January 1st van Gogh feels better and makes plans to send Gauguin's paintings to Paris.

Gauguin stays with the Schuffenecker family and begins to work on the series of zincographs (e.g. ill. 14) eventually presented at the Volpini exhibition.

Bernard in Paris works on his series of zincographs and shows them to Gauguin.

Bernard seeks exemption from military service.

Anquetin works in Etrépagny and takes care of his ailing mother.

FEBRUARY

Gauguin exhibits 12 paintings at the exhibition of *Les Vingt* in Brussels.

By mid-February van Gogh experiences mental suffering upon returning to his house.

MARCH-APRIL

Sometime in March or possibly early April, Gauguin departs for Pont-Aven.

On April 17th Théo marries Johanna Bonger.

MAY-JULY

Van Gogh, in early May, voluntarily commits himself to St. Paul's Hospital in St. Rémy.

In May Gauguin arrives back in Paris.

Sometime in late May-early June, the exhibition

"Groupe Impressionniste et Synthétiste" opens at the café of M. Volpini on the grounds of the World's Fair in Paris.

This is the first manifestation of the synthetist group of painters including Gauguin, Bernard, Laval, Anquetin and several other artists.

June 4th Gauguin leaves for Pont-Aven and spends two months with Meyer de Haan at the pension of Gloanec.

After seeing the Volpini exhibition, Paul Sérusier spends at least part of the summer in Pont-Aven.

In early July van Gogh receives the news that Théo's young wife is expecting.

AUGUST
Gauguin and Meyer de Haan spend the whole month in the coastal hamlet of Le Pouldu.

Bernard works in St. Briac and St. Malo.

Vincent is distressed because of his recurrent attacks and not being allowed to work out of doors.

SEPTEMBER
Théo is informed that Vincent has regained his lucidity of mind and that he has resumed painting.

Gauguin arrives in Pont-Aven.

Bernard is back in Paris.

OCTOBER-DECEMBER
In October, Lautrec exhibits in Paris his recently completed major canvas The Ball at the Moulin de la Galette (pl. 31) which is an immediate success.

Gauguin is back in Le Pouldu and resides with Meyer de Haan in the Inn of Mademoiselle Marie Henry. Here both artists decorate the dining room with wall paintings (pls. 16, 17) and hang paintings and graphics on the surrounding walls.

One of the most prolific periods of Gauguin's and Meyer de Haan's life begins.

Meyer de Haan apparently becomes the lover of Marie Henry and paints her portrait Motherhood (ill. 29).

Paul Sérusier joins Gauguin at Marie Henry's Inn for most of October.

Anquetin and Lautrec frequent the newly opened Dance Hall Moulin Rouge.

Bernard pays a visit to Théo's apartment in Paris in order to see van Gogh's recent canvases.

Van Gogh receives photographs of the recent works by Emile Bernard. He refutes these works as being too affected and abstract.

By December Bernard is working in Lille as a textile designer.

Sérusier in Paris begins in the winter 1889-90 to meet with the Nabi artists in the studio of Paul Ranson.

1890

JANUARY
The symbolist art critic Albert Aurier writes the pioneering exploratory critique on van Gogh's art in the French journal Mercure de France (Jan. 1).

January 31st Théo and Johanna's son Vincent Willem is born.

FEBRUARY
Gauguin returns from Le Pouldu to Paris uncertain that Meyer de Haan will be able to continue providing for their joint living expenses.

Gauguin stays in Paris until mid-June in the home of the Schuffenecker family, attempting to obtain governmental support for a trip to Tonkin.

Bernard struggles at being an industrial designer in Lille and writes to his friends of his deep moral despair. He experiences religious longings and hopes to go with Gauguin to Tonkin.

Lautrec exhibits The Ball at the Moulin de la Galette at the Les Vingt exhibition in Brussels.

Anquetin works in Paris on subjects from contemporary life in Paris.

MARCH
Van Gogh exhibits ten paintings at the exhibition Salon des Artistes Indépendants in Paris. Gauguin is struck by the importance of these works and suggests another exchange with Vincent.

MAY
Early in May van Gogh paints the Still Life: Vase with Irises.

Vincent leaves St. Paul's hospital in St. Rémy and travels to Paris to visit Théo and his wife and recently born young son.

On the 20th May he has arrived in his new lodgings in Auvers-sur-Oise where the artist begins to work and receives professional treatment from Dr. Paul Gachet.

JUNE
Vincent often dines at Dr. Gachet's home and works in the surrounding landscape at Auvers.

JULY
Van Gogh spends a Sunday in Paris at Théo's apartment where he lunches with Lautrec and sees Bernard.

July 27th, van Gogh shoots himself in the chest and dies on July 29th.

Bernard hears of the death of his friend and rushes to the latter's funeral accompanied by Charles Laval.

SEPTEMBER
Théo van Gogh, distressed by Vincent's death, experiences a sudden attack of paralysis and is replaced as manager of the Boussod and Valadon Gallery by Maurice Joyant, an old school friend of Lautrec.

1891

JANUARY
Théo falls ill and dies in Utrecht, The Netherlands on January 25th.

FEBRUARY
Around February 22nd, Bernard and his sister Madeleine encounter Gauguin at the latter's benefit sale of his paintings. An altercation arises over Gauguin's proclamation as the leader of symbolism. This is the last known contact between Bernard and Gauguin.

MARCH
Paintings by Lautrec, van Gogh, Anquetin are shown at the Salon des Artistes Indépendants in Paris.

Gauguin is given a testimonial banquet by the Symbolist poets at the Café Voltaire in Paris.

Albert Aurier proclaims Gauguin the representative of symbolism in his definitive article on the artist's work (Mercure de France, March 1).

APRIL
Gauguin departs for Tahiti on April 4th.

AUTUMN
Lautrec creates his first lithographic poster, At the Moulin Rouge: La Goulue.

DECEMBER
Paintings by Bernard, Anquetin, Gauguin, van Gogh, Lautrec are exhibited at the first exhibition of "Peintres Impressionnistes et Symbolistes" at the Gallery of Le Barc de Boutteville in Paris.